BETTER JOB FASTER

Claudia Jordan

WorkLife Publishing
Phoenix, Arizona

Published by:
WorkLife Publishing
4532 E. Grandview Rd.
Phoenix, AZ 85032
Phone: (602) 992-0144 Fax: (602) 493-9321

Library of Congress Catalog Card Number: 97-61928

Publishers Cataloging-in-Publication Data
Jordan, Claudia
     JobFinder: How to Find a Better Job Faster / Claudia Jordan
     Includes index.
     Bibliography.
     1. Job hunting
     2. Career identification
     3. Job satisfaction
     4. Employment interviewing
     ISBN 0-9653868-4-8

Printed by Affiliated Lithograph in the United States of America

Cover design by Mark LaLone
Photograph of author by Steve Thompson

To my husband for his unlimited support, encouragement and love.

Special thanks to my editor, Gwen Henson, for her patience, endless readings and insightful suggestions.

Contents

Part I: Target Your Job Search

Part II: Market Yourself to Success

Part III: Interview to Get Job Offers

Appendix A: What Do You Want to Be?

Appendix B: Resources

How To Find A
BETTER JOB FASTER

Claudia Jordan

PART I

Target Your Job Search

He knew he had to act quickly. Everything was at stake. His whole life was hanging from a shoestring. Tiny beads of sweat popped out on his forehead as John punched in the number of the taxi company on his cell phone. "Send a cab right away! This is urgent!" He loosened his tie and paced the floor, glancing out the window every few minutes.

When the cab arrived, John sprinted out the front door, down the steps, and into the back seat. He slammed the door and yelled, "Get going! What are you waiting for?"

"Ya right...so where's the fire?" the driver scowled as the yellow cab leaped forward. Silence. He glanced in the rear view mirror. "Hey buddy, where are you goin' in such a rush?"

"Well, I'm not sure...if you would just drive around I'll know it when I see it. But I need to get there right away—I don't have much time."

"Aw, come on buddy! Give me a clue—north, east, south, or west?"

"Let's see...I used to like downtown, but forget that! I want something different. I went to the mountains once, and it was okay." John reached in his briefcase and handed the cabby a sheet of paper. "Here's all the places I've been. Maybe you can figure it out."

"Sure buddy, whatever. It's your money."

———

Unfortunately, many job searches are conducted in this manner. People urgently create a great deal of frantic energy—applying for jobs, sending letters and resumes, and interviewing—all for positions they hope might fit them somehow. After a while the rejection and the silence weigh heavily—and into the downward spiral job seekers fall. Even when you know your destination, getting there, and getting there quickly, can be difficult.

Today, it's tougher than ever to find a good job. But success is the reward for those who are prepared and understand how the job market works. Success goes to those who know the most about how to get hired. That means identifying and targeting the best work for your unique abilities and desires AND using the most effective job search techniques to land that job. Don't think, however, you have to keep doing the same old thing. Not by a long shot. Change is good, and adapting to the new job market is imperative. To find success you must present your talents effectively for your ideal job target. You must identify your ideal job target first, then go out and get that job.

Or you could always call a taxi.

Three Keys to Find a Better Job Faster

1. **Target your job search.**
2. **Market yourself successfully.**
3. **Interview to get job offers.**

"Great!" you might say, "...but just how do I do all of that?"

The JOBFINDER series—books, tapes, and action planner—is designed to guide you through the perils of the job search, quickly and effectively, so you come out a winner. Why settle for a second-rate, boring or stressful, and often low-paying job when your ideal job is within reach?

2

I *guarantee* if you follow the simple steps outlined in this book your job search will be a proactive, rewarding, and enriching experience that will make a positive impact in the quality of your life. Now *that* is worth spending some time and effort.

Many people look for a job backwards. First, they start looking for job openings, then they try to see which available job they can fit themselves into. To find the job you are most capable of—that uses the best of you—first you must define exactly what you want, then go out and look for that particular kind of work.

Your Specific Dream
+ Burning Desire
+ Planned Actions
= Rewarding Worklife.

STEP 1

Visualize and Define Your Next Job

If you were granted any job that you are qualified for, what would it be? Once you are able to visualize your next job in detail, it's much easier to find it and to get the offer. Plus your excitement, confidence, and optimistic attitude—all highly desired traits in an employee—will be obvious to the employer.

Start with an open mind and positive thoughts. Begin to think about an ideal job you could do now, preferably one that's a bit challenging and a bit scary.

Let's start when you wake up and dress for your new ideal job. What do you wear?

Now visualize yourself entering your workplace. What kind of building is it? Or do you work outdoors?

What kind of people are your co-workers, boss, customers, and people you interface with?

Are you working with people, plants, or animals?

Do you work with tools, materials, equipment, instruments, machinery, electronic gadgets, or food?

Do you use information found in books, computers, maps, blueprints, files, manuals, reports, newspapers, periodicals, etc.?

Describe the kind of work are you doing all day.

What accomplishments do you hope to achieve during your first six months?

After you have given some thought to these questions, it's time to write down the answers. It's important to record your visualization so you can read it often and embed it deeper in your mind. Write in the present tense, as if it were happening right now, such as, "I wake up at dawn and put on my blue jeans..." Take your time and lavish it with details. Do it now, please.

Can you answer this question? I am looking for a job as a _____ in the _____ field. If you answered it without hesitation, then congratulations! You are ready to begin your job search.

If you couldn't answer positively or had trouble visualizing your job in the previous exercise, you need to do more work before you begin your job search. Knowing exactly what you want is half the battle of finding a better job faster. Remember the guy anxiously calling the taxi? Don't put yourself in that position. Determining what you want now will save you weeks and months of frustration, and even years should you settle for the wrong job. Please turn to Appendix A, "What Do You Want to Be?" and do the exercises.

The most effective way to target your next job is to describe it by function and industry. Function describes what you do, and industry identifies the products or services of your work. Expressing your desired work in these terms will clearly communicate your job objective while allowing you flexibility. Job titles are usually too limiting, and not having an objective at all leaves you floundering like a fish out of water. What will you say when people ask what you want to do?

Here are some examples:

Job Descriptions by Function/Industry

Function	Industry
Publicist	Literary Arts
Salesperson	Fine Jewelry
Investigator	Medical Insurance Claims
Office Manager	Health Care Organization
Interior Designer	Corporate Offices
Purchasing	Hotels & Resorts
Electrician	Custom Homes
General Director	Tennis & Golf Sporting Events
Project Director	Housing Development
Technical Writer	Computers/Electronics
Chemist	Pharmaceutical Research Lab
Editorial Assistant	Fashion Magazine

Function	Industry
Trip Leader	Wilderness Expeditions
Manager	Restaurant
Security Manager	Government
Translator	French/Spanish/German

Now describe **your next job** by function/industry.

I want a job as a _____ in the _____ field.

My second choice is a job as a _____ in the _____ field.

For more help in choosing your favorite industry, turn to Appendix A, Step E for a list of industries. If you have trouble determining your function, turn to Appendix A, and do the exercises. It really works! It's better to spend a few hours now figuring out what you want to be than to blunder through your job search wasting precious time and money. The time you spend unemployed or in the wrong job can cost you a bundle of money and distress.

The following table illustrates the degree of change from your past work to your new work. The greater the change, the more work you must do to make the change successful. Which one fits your situation?

1. Same industry, same function	3. Same industry, different function
2. Same function, different industry	4. Different industry, different function

Box 1: Your next job is basically the same as your past work. You probably have contacts in your industry and know the names of businesses you want to work for.

Box 2: Your new work will be the same function (such as sales), but the industry will change (i.e., from computers to medical equipment).

Box 3: Your new work is the same industry, but your function will change (i.e., money management from loan officer to financial planner).

Box 4: Complete change of industry and function.

Obviously, the first situation will be the easiest to accomplish. In the second and third situations you will carry over many transferable skills and knowledge to your new work. The fourth situation is the most difficult to change to, but far from impossible. It just requires more work and time. In each situation, *the most important quality is your attitude and desire.* If you *believe* your new work is perfect for you, and *you want it* more than anything, you will work harder to get it and be more excited in the process. It's the first step on the path of success.

STEP 2

Calculate Your Qualifications

From this point on, you should be thinking and marketing yourself in terms of what the employer wants, NOT what you want. Keep your preferences to yourself—the employer doesn't care what you want until hiring time.

For a moment put yourself in your next employer's shoes. You're the boss and you have to hire the best candidate to fill a position as a _____ (the same position you want) in the _____ industry. Name the five most challenging tasks of this position:

1. _____
2. _____
3. _____
4. _____
5. _____

As the employer, you need someone who has the best skills to solve these challenging tasks. The top five skills the best candidate will have for this position are:

1. _____
2. _____
3. _____
4. _____
5. _____

Is it necessary to have a degree, special education, training or certification to perform this job? If so, name it.

Personality and attitude are also very important on the job. The ideal candidate would have the following personal characteristics: (For example, motivated, accurate, organized. See Appendix B for more examples.)

1._____
2._____
3._____
4._____
5._____

You've just described what the employer wants. Now let's determine what you have to offer that's most relevant to what the employer wants. Keep uppermost in your mind what the employer is looking for. Your brain surgeon experience doesn't help if the employer wants a chef.

Your job target: (by function/industry)
Your top five skills for this job:

1._____
2._____
3._____
4._____
5._____

Your top five characteristics for this job:

1._____
2._____
3._____
4._____
5._____

Next, list your education, training, certifications or licences relevant to your job target.

These skills, characteristics, and education are your qualifications for this job. (Refer to the list of Personal Characteristics in Appendix B for more help.) Your job target plus your qualifications are the **key communication** in your job search from your resume to phone calls to networking to interviewing.

Do not underestimate the power of attitude in your job search and as part of your qualifications. At a two-day job search seminar for trainers, we, the attendees, were given an assignment during our lunch hour. We had to call or visit a business and ask the manager: "What is the single most important quality you look for when you're hiring?" We compared notes back at the seminar and the answer from an overwhelming 90 percent of the sixty employers was: *Attitude!*

Once you've identified your job target and your best qualifications for that job (skills and characteristics), you have a superior foundation from which to launch your job search.

If you are finding it difficult to name your job target or your top skills and characteristics, please turn to Appendix A in the back of the book and—you know the drill—do the exercises.

STEP 3

Create a Targeted Resume

Think of your resume as a marketing tool—a product brochure. You're marketing a special and rare product—YOU! Specifically your abilities, skills, education, characteristics, experience, values, and everything that comprises your uniqueness to fulfill a specific job.

A resume is necessary for two reasons: 1) Everyone will ask you for one, and 2) A well-written resume will help you target your job search. By organizing your thoughts and accomplishments, it will enable you to communicate effectively, and it will broadcast to potential employers exactly what you want and why they should hire you.

But please remember: Your resume is not a magic wand that will conjure up a job for you. Use your resume as a powerful tool to HELP in your search—not as a magic spell to do all the work and find a job for you. Stories abound about people who sent out mass mailings of resumes and failed miserably. Or people who sent their resume to every want ad that was even remotely within their realm—and failed miserably. These two techniques are not targeting your job search—these methods are like throwing spaghetti against the wall to see if anything sticks and if not, throwing more and more until one tiny little noodle clings to the wall, and then desperately grabbing it. You'll find more about marketing in the next chapter.

The most effective way to get an interview is to talk to people face-to-face. The second most effective method is by telephone, and the least successful way is by sending something through the mail or a computer service. The less human contact, the lower your chances.

Two good ways to use your resume are to send it ahead to preface a meeting or leave it after a meeting for reinforcement. Sometimes your resume may compete with numerous other resumes, or it may simply contend for the potential employer's time. However you use your resume, it's important to make it (and you) stand out.

How do you ensure that your resume gets noticed? Or gets read? Even if you're leaving your resume after a meeting, an excellent one will enhance your chances. Every contact with a potential employer is a chance to make a good impression and *demonstrate your skills*. Take full advantage of these opportunities!

An outstanding resume must look exceptional from the first ten-second glance. It should be laser printed on quality stationery (one page preferred), with wide margins and a well-organized format, with bulleted statements or small paragraphs for easy reading. While good looks are necessary, they can be deceiving—superior content will ultimately hold the employer's attention.

Crucial Resume Elements

- **Job Target** (expressed by function/industry)
- **Profile** (your specific qualifications for your job target)
- **Accomplishments** (relevant to your job target)
- **Skills** (relevant to your job target)

If your resume passes the first glance of its overall appearance, then the employer will look for *something* that tells what you want to do—objective, job title, summary, or profile. The employer does not have time to figure out what you want to do. If you don't know, or haven't taken the time to find out, why are you wasting the employer's time (and yours)? If you state your objective in a cover letter instead, your resume will still be hopelessly generic—the kiss of death—speeding its way to the circular file. Describing what you want by industry/function allows you flexibility while telling the employer your objective in a glance.

Still scanning, the employer will concentrate on the top half of your resume. This is prime space. A well-written targeted profile describing your top qualifications—corresponding to the company's top needs—is **POWERFUL**. These qualifications and capabilities show potential employers what you can do for them **now**—the perfect bridge from your past to your future. Your profile showcases your unique talents and character. Most job seekers badly neglect this area of their resume, so yours will stand out like an oasis in the desert. Your profile will also play a major role in marketing yourself through networking, using the telephone, and writing letters.

If your resume passes the scan test, the employer is interested enough to read on. The rest of your resume backs up your qualifications with facts and figures, concisely outlining your accomplishments. It targets the work you want to do next, because it only contains data relevant to your job target—everything else is eliminated. The potential employer doesn't want to read about the years you were a dog trainer when you are applying for a position as a financial analyst. (However you could emphasize the business management end instead of the dog training.)

If you have completed the exercises from Appendix A, you have all the material needed to create your very own unique, targeted resume. All it needs is organization and polish.

Let's begin with each segment of an outstanding resume. Get your computer or pad and pen ready.

1. Heading

Include your name, address, and phone number(s). An answering machine, dependable answering service, or voice mail is a must. Make it easy to reach you or leave a message—potential employers will call only once. Don't use a post office box address—it looks transient. Generally, your name should be written "friendly," such as Jerry Higgins rather than Gerald Bartholomew Higgins. It makes you seem more approachable. A formal position requires a more formal name, such as Gerald B. Higgins, M.D. Avoid cutesy nicknames like "Chip" or "Candy." Insert a line after your heading to separate your contact information from your resume. It creates a cleaner, appealing look.

2. Job Target/Objective/Profession/Expertise

The idea is to communicate to the employer what you want to do while allowing you flexibility. This is accomplished beautifully by simply stating your function and industry, followed by your profile or qualifications for the job. To show the level of the position you are seeking use terms like "executive level, upper management, managerial position, supervisory position, team leadership, or senior _____." The scope of specific titles like Manager and Vice President varies greatly from large to small companies, and they should be avoided unless you change them for each company. Do not use "entry level," because you may sell yourself short before you even begin! Make a separate resume for each job target and you will be rewarded for the extra effort.

DO NOT MAKE A RESUME WITHOUT A JOB TARGET. If you don't know your job target, turn to Appendix A in the back, and do the exercises. Looking for a job without a target is like going on vacation without a destination—your chances of ending up somewhere fantastic are incredibly bleak. And please, don't insult the employer's intelligence (and yours) with a weak objective like this: "Seeking a challenging position with a growing company which will utilize my education and experience." So what? Who wants a stagnant position with a downsizing company using skills and training you don't have?

3. Profile/Qualifications

These are *your best qualifications to perform your job target*—and the qualifications *employers are looking for*. The profile may include credentials, education, accomplishments, skills, capabilities, and personality traits—a thumbnail sketch of why they should hire you or at least consider you as a top candidate. Review the list you made of the skills and characteristics your *next employer* will be looking for. Now review *your* best skills and characteristics for this job target. Try to match the employer's list as much as possible. Then write out five or six lines describing these qualities. Before each sentence imagine a silent "I am..." or "I can..." or "I have..."

The profile is best written in bullet style, or it can be a paragraph with four or five lines, but the bullet style is more likely to be read. This section can be difficult to write, so to begin just jot down the main points that come to mind and return later to perfect it.

Sample Profiles With Job Targets
Profession: Registered Nurse, Health Care Services
Profile
- Ability to remain calm, follow procedures, and provide correct assessments during stressful situations.
- Communicate well with patients, family members, doctors, and staff.
- Professional, competent, and effective team member.
- More than fifteen years experience in providing quality health care.

———

Objective: Medical Malpractice Claims Representative
Highlights of Qualifications
- Nine years experience as a claims representative for medical malpractice and casualty/property claims.
- Excel in thoroughness of investigation, liability evaluation, and determining case value.
- Skilled in successful negotiation and interaction with attorneys; considerable litigation and trial experience.
- Extensive knowledge of technical aspects in the medical field.

———

Objective: Event Management for professional sporting events
Qualifications
- Ten years experience in managing all aspects of successful major sporting events.
- Expert in establishing effective priorities, delegating authority, and maintaining detailed, on-time work schedules and projects.

- Adept at recruiting, building, and energizing a productive team.
- Effectively negotiate sponsor agreements and provide specialized services.
- Exceptionally good at solving problems and handling emergencies; ability to work well under pressure.

———

Job Target: Vehicle Wholesale Operation Manager
Qualifications
- Proven ability to maintain cost effective operations.
- Excellent interpersonal and communication skills.
- Work effectively with customers, employees, and management.
- Organized, professional, and dedicated to the job.
- Extensive background in complete wholesale management.
- Willing to relocate, available to work overseas, current passport.

———

Expertise: Public Relations/Business Management/Real Estate
Profile
- Enthusiastic, energetic, and polished professional with strong interpersonal skills and a willingness to "go the extra mile."
- Accomplished in promoting public relations.
- Master's talent for planning and directing major events.
- Establish and maintain an important cadre of business and social contacts.
- Expert in business, property, and financial management.

———

Job Target: Front office or managerial position in a dental office
Profile
- Lifelong enthusiasm and thirteen years experience in the dental field.
- Competent in financial management, insurance billing, and administrative tasks.
- Extremely organized and detail oriented.

• Dependable, trustworthy professional with a knack for making people feel at ease and comfortable.

———

Objective: Director of Maintenance for Lincoln School District
Qualification Profile
- More than ten years successful experience in maintenance, construction, and custodial management.
- Proven track record in planning, bidding, and supervision of projects on schedule and under budget.
- Highly competent manager and administrator with ability to motivate employees to perform at their best.
- Degree in Transportation Management; B.S. in Business Administration.

———

Objective: Human Resources/Community Services
Summary of Qualifications
- Expertise in developing positive working relationships with civic organizations, the community, and members of the media.
- Extensive training and experience in personnel matters, problem solving, and issue resolution.
- Achievement in operations management, human resource development, information systems coordination, budget planning and implementation.
- Recognized throughout career for creative, employee-oriented administration; possess exceptional communications skills.

———

Objective: Optometry or ophthalmology assistant
Profile
- Compassionate professional dedicated to providing the finest vision care and training.
- Certified Optometric Vision Therapist, Technician, and Assistant.
- Excel in organizing and supervising programs, committees, special projects, and business offices.

•Able to instill confidence, loyalty, and trust in patients.
•Extensive knowledge and lifelong enthusiasm in the optometry and health care field.

4. Experience

Start with your last or present job and go back about ten years. More or fewer is acceptable if it's to your benefit and relevant to your target. List your job title, name of company, city and state, and years worked. Months are not necessary—they add clutter, plus it's easier to cover small gaps between jobs. (Exception: Summer jobs for students.) List the dates after the company name, not in the left-hand column where they waste valuable space. What you did is more important than how long you worked there. If it's relevant, list volunteer work just as you would a job, but you don't have to mention that it's volunteer work. After all, you gain experience whether you're paid or not.

5. Accomplishments

Under each job heading, list your accomplishments from that job that *relate to your new job target.* Do not make a boring list of your responsibilities and duties. The employer wants to know *how you performed your job and the results of your actions.* These statements should back up or prove your qualifications for your job target. A simple way for you to identify accomplishments is to think like this:

PROBLEM→ ACTIONS→ RESULTS

Accomplishments are things you have done that create value, often improving the profitability of the company such as:
•Generated revenue
•Cut costs
•Saved time
•Increased productivity
•Improved customer service
•Motivated, trained, or taught others
•Invented or created
•Improved quality
•Used technology

For instance, an accomplishment might be, "Restructured filing system." So what? Why did you do it? What were the results and benefits? Rewrite as, "Restructured filing system streamlining retrieval of files and saving five hours of filing per week." The benefit of saving time translates to saving money for the company.

Use figures whenever possible to show your scope of accomplishment or skill, but use the figures to your advantage. If you increased business revenues from $50K to $65K, it's more impressive to say, "Increased business revenues by 30 percent in one year." On the other hand if you increased the revenues by 30 percent but you started at $995,000 and went to $1,298,000, it's better to express it in the million dollar figures because the scope of your responsibility is much larger. It would sound more impressive if you round it off to "...from $1 million to $1.3 million."

Instead of saying "Supervised staff," be more specific to project a clearer image. Use "Supervised engineering department of twelve people," or "Supervised staff of four managers, two administrative assistants, twenty-two salespeople, and two warehouse workers."

For clarity, express numbers this way: $77,000 instead of $77K; $200 million instead of $200,000,000 or $200MM; and USA$200 million to express the figure in United States dollars. Generally write out numbers one through ten and use the numeric form for 11 and above. There are exceptions to these rules—know and use the norm in your field.

For your accomplishment statements, begin each sentence with an action verb, eliminating "I" or "we." A list of action verbs and more help identifying your accomplishments is in the accomplishment section in Appendix A.

If you have completed the appendix, from your accomplishment worksheets choose the achievements you enjoyed the most and that *support your objective*. Condense each one into a one-liner but tell what actions you took and what the *results and benefits* were.

Don't agonize over this step until you're paralyzed. Just write statements out to get your thoughts down, then continue to move forward. It's much easier to come back to condense and revise later.

6. Education and Training

List education after experience, unless your education is more important than your experience. Include degrees, schools, city, and state—the year graduated is optional. Also include seminars, training, certificates, and licenses *relevant to your job target.* You can mention a degree or license in the Profile/Qualifications section, and list the details here. If you are a recent grad, go into more details about your school activities and accomplishments.

7. Organizations, Associations, and More

List only those affiliations and associations that support your job target and are non-controversial. Include officer or committee designations, if any.

Do not state "References available upon request"—as if you wouldn't provide them if asked! You will automatically provide them at all good interviews and will prepare them on a separate page later.

Don't mention personal information such as marital status, children, age, health, or hobbies. Don't mention salary history or reasons for leaving any job, and NEVER lie. Don't give the employer a needless reason to eliminate you.

These "rules" are guidelines to create the most effective targeted resume. You can break a rule, but you should have a *very strong reason* for doing so, and it must make sense.

Choose a Format

There are two basic types of resumes—chronological and functional. A chronological resume is the traditional resume, which is organized by jobs, while the functional resume is organized by functions. The easiest method is to create a chronological resume first, then if you determine a functional resume is best, you can easily switch by organizing the sentences under different functions. You have compiled the preceding information in a chronological format.

The functional resume is well-suited for career changes, covering patchy work history, adding spice to the same job you've had for years, or describing the same type of work you've performed in several jobs. It is more difficult to write, but if done well, can be very effective in translating your skills and achievements to fit your new job or career. (See sample functional resumes on pages 35-37.)

In the past, functional resumes had a bad reputation with many employers because they left out vital information: the years worked, companies, and the positions held. This obstacle is overcome with a chronological Experience History section.

First, name three or four of the most important main functions necessary to perform your job target—they should be the main activities the employer is seeking. Use these functions as the main headings under Experience. Select accomplishments from your past jobs and list them under the appropriate function, regardless of which job, volunteer work, or leisure activity it was from.

Examples:
(Objective: Sporting Event Management)
Marketing and Promoting
- Successfully bartered with vendors to obtain gifts, materials, and services for events, players, and sponsors.
- Prepared and directed opening-night ceremonies and awards presentations for live television coverage; coordinated live and taped radio promotions.
- Initiated local community involvement through contests, numerous social events, and support of charities.
- Directed design and distribution of printed promotional materials: ticket brochures, newspaper ads, posters, detail sheets, counter boards, and flyers.

———

(Objective: List and market lender-owned properties)
Residential Sales
- Rank in top 10 percent of company's sales force (850 agents).
- Sell over $7 million in residential real estate annually.
- Sold more than 875 homes in last twelve years.
- Ability to negotiate until mutually agreeable terms are met.
- Well versed in the legal aspects of real estate.

23

(Objective: Senior level trainer in life management skills)
Leadership and Training
- Directed internship training program for nine years.
- Trained groups and leaders in start-up and establishment of four new organizations.
- Senior level leadership in organization which grew from 250 to 800 members.
- Recruited and trained 120 leaders of on-going groups dealing with life management issues.
  —Oversaw training groups of 100-200 people per year.
  —Designed curriculum for classes in conflict resolution, counseling skills, communication skills, small group interaction, and time management.
  —Strengthened and saved many marriages and families throughout program.

The last example shows how to handle complex information. Did you guess it was the resume of a former minister looking for job outside the church? *The language was changed to universal business language,* and a two-page format was used to list his employment history on the second page. This way potential employers won't automatically dismiss him when they see his previous profession. This method effectively deals with career changers. It also illustrates how to communicate your transferable skills during your job search.

For the Employment History or Experience History section, simply list years worked, title, and company with city and state. Include volunteer work if it fits your situation. If there are large gaps, fill in the reason such as child rearing, special studies, travel, or a sabbatical. Arrange the list in columns to make it easy to read.

The objective/job target line, the profile section, and the education area remain the same as in a chronological resume.

Voila! You have just created a well-written functional resume.

Polish Your Resume

Now that you've finished the first draft of your resume and have arranged it in a format, it's time to polish it until it gleams.

Most important is to fit it on one page. Editing will force you to pare down the text to the most important facts and make every word tell. A one-page, well-edited resume encourages employers to read your resume and understand it. (Not that!) You will give more details later during the interview. That's the idea, isn't it? Of course, the one-page rule can be broken, but your resume absolutely should not exceed two pages, with the main points listed on the first page.

Begin each sentence with an action verb like managed, designed, trained, etc. Using verbs helps you cut words and makes your resume come alive. If you're referring to a current job, put it in present tense like supervise, create, etc. Refer to the action verb list in the appendix for help. Use each action verb only once in your resume to avoid boring repetition. Once I read a resume with the word "managed" repeated eighteen times! A thesaurus is invaluable and available at the library if you don't own one.

Use vocabulary that you would naturally use. Some business jargon is necessary to show your expertise, but don't overdo it. The average business person should be able to understand what you do from reading your resume.

Be consistent in style, format, and organization. Use the same type of headings for the same type of data, and make sure it's simple for the reader to pick out specific facts at a glance. Is it easy to find dates, titles, education, and achievements?

Now your resume must be typeset. If you're using a computer, you can do it yourself. Choose a conservative typestyle but not one like Courier that looks like an old typewriter—you'll look helplessly outdated. Avoid the temptation to over format: use bold, italics, caps, and small caps sparingly. Generally avoid underlining—it's old fashioned—and use italics for emphasis. The size of the letters should make it easy to read (without a magnifying glass!) even when faxed. Use a minimum of one inch side margins and one-half inch top and bottom margins. If your resume still doesn't fit on one page, condense and cut more text.

If you don't have a computer or want professional help creating your resume, you have several options. You can use a resume service or desktop publishing service, both found in the yellow page phone directory. They can help you write it, critique it, and condense it,

25

if necessary, plus typeset and print your resume. Copy/print shops offer typesetting and printing. However, they will only typeset exactly what you give them.

Please note the difference between *printing* and *copying.* If you have access to a computer and a laser or ink jet printer you can print your resume. Or take a high quality master copy to a print/copy shop and have it copied on a quality photocopier, or have it printed. Copying is acceptable if you start with a good original. Do not use colored inks or colored paper. Stick with black ink on conservative white, buff, or light gray paper. Use a high quality paper. A large variety of paper and envelopes is available at your local print shop. This stationery can be purchased in any quantity. To save money, go to a large office supply or a paper store to buy a ream of paper (500 sheets).

Cover letters, marketing letters, envelopes, references, and thank you letters should all be on matching stationery (covered in Part II). Mailing your resume in a white 9 x 12-inch envelope looks more impressive, and it usually gets opened first, but remember that the postage may be more.

Should you have others critique your resume? Yes and no. Definitely have several people check it for spelling, typos, and grammar. In regard to content, everyone will respond differently. What matters is what potential employers think of it. Having several professionals in your preferred field review it is helpful—if they have experience in reviewing resumes. Even then, don't change it unless you are given a compelling reason or several people have made the same point.

Sample Resumes

The sample resumes on the following pages illustrate proficient, interview-winning resumes. They are designed to pass the "scan test" and capture the attention and respect of the employer. Use them as guidelines.

Jennifer Peters
1306 E. Larkspur, Scottsdale, AZ 85254 •(602) 992-5612

OBJECTIVE: Sales position in real estate.

PROFILE
- Excel in client/customer interaction at all levels.
- Six years real estate experience, ten years in customer service.
- Professional, articulate, detail oriented.
- Arizona Real Estate License, member Scottsdale Board of Realtors.

EXPERIENCE
Contract Administrator, Desert Hills, Inc.
Phoenix, AZ 1992-present
- Oversee real estate contract process from initiation to closing.
- Interface with buyer, sales staff, sales manager, title company, and legal department.
- Assist sales staff in greeting prospective purchasers, providing project information, and developing rapport.

Office Manager, Red Lyon Development Group
Phoenix, AZ 1990-92
- Promoted to Office Manager after three months as secretary.
- Assisted in management of numerous limited and general partnerships.
- Handled correspondence for executives, coordinated special projects for salespeople, performed bookkeeping duties.

Customer Service, various restaurants
Scottsdale, AZ 1986-90
- Self-supported through college as food waitress and bartender.
- Received several rapid promotions, trained staff, assisted in restaurant operations, and supervised personnel.

EDUCATION
Arizona Real Estate License, 1994
Scottsdale Community College, Scholarship, Deans Honor
     List, 1984-89

Susan A. Hensley

1832 N. Catalina Dr., Tempe, Arizona (602) 478-9362

Objective: Mortgage Banking Management

Highlights of Qualifications:
- Outstanding leadership skills, an effective manager able to energize a crew, roll up sleeves and pitch in when needed.
- Knowledgeable in all phases of mortgage banking.
- Excel in developing harmonious customer relations in retail and wholesale lending.
- Committed to producing results beyond what's expected.

Professional Experience
Branch Manager
Franklin Mortgage Company, Phoenix, AZ 1995-1996
- Direct development of residential mortgages, processing and closing procedures, accounting department, and staff of fifteen.
- Involved in start-up of company which evolved from Ben Franklin Mortgage Co.

Senior Vice President
Benjamin Franklin Mortgage Company, Scottsdale, AZ 1990-1995
- Instrumental in start-up and on-going operation of company; number one lender in Maricopa County in 1993 and 1994.
- Directed and co-directed all aspects of mortgage lending end operations from loan production to loan closing/shipping.
- Loan production of company more than $200 million annually.
- Ensured all loans met turnaround time and clients were served in an efficient, professional manner.
- Effectively managed growth of staff from three to sixty.
- Personal loan approval up to $300,000.
- Supervised accounting department; proficient in procedures.
- Opened and relocated ten offices in four years, all on schedule.

Previous Experience
Loan Sales Supervisor, Merabank; Corporate Collector, American Express; retail credit and finance positions.

Education
B.S. Business Administration, Major: Finance. Mankato State University, MN

Jake Brickman
2315 East Broadway Road • Tempe, AZ 85066 • 602-431-1795

Profession: Purchasing/Electronics

Profile
- Excel in purchasing, sourcing, and meeting tight delivery schedules.
- Proven record of negotiating best costs to ensure profitability.
- Maintain excellent business relationships with local electronics and associated components suppliers.
- Extensive Pacific Rim purchasing experience.
- Ability to interface well with engineering, manufacturing, quality assurance, and finance areas.
- Degreed electronics professional, current computer systems literate.

Professional Experience
Purchasing Manager, Hypercom, Inc. Phoenix, AZ (1993 to present)
EFT Telecommunications, Credit Card Terminals/Network Equipment
- Purchased, received, and supplied $3.6 million of materials for production of equipment in past year.
- Consistently purchased material 8 to 15 percent lower than industry standards.
- Project Leader for new terminal model, mold design, production molding, and modification. Saved over $200,000 in production costs while meeting short delivery schedules for 10,000 systems.
- Continuously provided material for ten day turnaround of prototype PCBs.
- Sourced and managed quick turn mass production of 500 terminal PCBs within five weeks, including parts kitting of 230 parts.

Vice President, Semi-Systems Arizona, Inc. Phoenix, AZ (1986-92)
- Cultivated sales growth of new company to $5 million per year.
- Developed local distribution sales for represented components.
- Established relationships with local representatives. and distributors.

Previous Experience
Technical Publications Manager (Motorola), Technical Writer, Electronics Technician

Education
AEE Degree, DeVry Technical Institute of Technology, Chicago, IL

Jennifer Warner
4555 Kiva Street, Scottsdale, AZ 85054 • (602) 988-4313

Objective: Teacher, in grades K-8.

Profile:
- Ability to make learning a pleasure rather than a duty.
- Excel in using creative, alternative teaching methods.
- Enthusiastic, responsible, mature, with strong desire to teach children.
- Four years experience in teaching and working with children.
- Well versed with Macintosh and Apple computers, and arts and crafts.

Education: BA Liberal Arts. Major, history; minor, English. Arizona State University, Phoenix, AZ 1995
- Expected Masters of Education in 1998
- Seminars attended: Child Molestation, Control in the Classroom
- Certified in first aid and CPR training

Experience:

Teacher/Life Skills Coordinator, 1994-present
Scottsdale Boys and Girls Club, Scottsdale, AZ
- Design, organize, and teach courses to children ages five to ten:

  -Self-esteem -Swimming   -Survival Skills -Computers
  -Home skills -Theater   -Careers   -Crafts
  -Fashion   -Journalism   -Drug & Alcohol Awareness
- Coordinate monthly newsletter program.
- Organize teachers lesson plans, obtain speakers, and plan field-trips.

Teacher's Aide, 1992-1994
Kiva Public School, Paradise Valley, AZ
- Originated rewarding programs such as Artist's Corner and Author's Chair within a Special Education classroom, grades one through four.
- Designed bulletin boards, graded class assignments, and provided personal assistance for children.
- Observed IEP parent/teacher conferences.

Head Camp Counselor, Summer 1991
Easter Seals Handicamp, Idaho Springs, CO
- Developed programs for 15 mentally and physically challenged adults and children. Supervised two counselors.

Sales Associate, 1990-1992, Robinson's Department Store

Doug McNally
465 S. Dobson Rd., Chandler, AZ 85065   602-983-7905

JOB TARGET: Sales or Sales Management for a manufacturer.

PROFILE
- Twelve years experience producing high volume sales for manufacturers.
- Excel in expanding customer base by acquiring major customers and opening new markets.
- Ability to work well with management, engineering, and sales staff.
- Excellent contract negotiator.
- Dedicated, trustworthy, and highly motivated professional able to resolve problems and get the job done.

EXPERIENCE
Manufacturer's Representative
Self-employed, Phoenix, AZ 1992-present
- Helped build a $4 million business from $300,000 as sales rep.
- Produced sales for sheetmetal house that grew to five times its original size during my tenure.
- Expanded customer bases while maintaining existing bases, acquired major accounts, improved quality control standards, negotiated major contracts, and worked with engineering staffs on various projects.
- Represented casting and sheet metal companies, circuit board manufacturers, and machine shops in Arizona, New Mexico, and California.
- Major accounts included Motorola, Sperry-Honeywell, Garrett, etc.

VP Marketing and Sales
Treffers Precision, Phoenix, AZ 1990-92
- Built annual company sales from $720,000 to $3.6 million in two years.
- Initiated aggressive marketing campaign, supervised sales staff of 19, assisted in reorganizing company.

Systems Analyst, Whitney Aircraft Company, Middletown, CT, 1988-90
Salesman, Precision Plating, Garden Grove, CA, 1985-88

EDUCATION
B.S. Aeronautical Engineering Technology, Northrop University, 1985

OTHER: Held Secret Security Clearance, current licensed pilot.

KURT JAIMES
1606 W. Camelback Rd., Phoenix, AZ 85033 (602) 951-8656

OBJECTIVE: Retail/Small Business Management

PROFILE
- Aggressive professional with strong desire and ability to exceed goals.
- Effective in recruiting, training, and energizing a high-performance team.
- Resourceful, committed, and enthusiastic self-starter with excellent communication skills, written and oral.
- Proven track record in small business management with emphasis on customer service and the bottom line.

PROFESSIONAL EXPERIENCE
General Manager/Owner, 1995-96
T.A.G. Real Estate Investors, Little Rock, AR
- Conducted market research, evaluated properties, negotiated purchases, and supervised improvements.
- Marketed and sold properties with average ROI of 50 percent.

Sales and Operations Manager/Co-Owner, 1990-95
Different Seasons (home furnishings retail business), Little Rock, AR
- Instrumental in start-up and establishment of retail business. Directed growth of company from $650,000 to $1.6 million in revenues.
- Managed 25 employees. Recruited, interviewed, hired, and trained store managers, assistants, bookkeepers, and sales staff.
- Conducted financial analysis audit and cut expenses by $175,000 while maintaining company objectives.
- Developed detailed sales forecasts and annual cash flow requirements. Initiated sales incentive programs to achieve goals.
- Implemented computer accounting system, saving substantial accounting fees. Handled accounts receivable/payable, general ledger, and payroll.

District Sales Manager, 1989-90
Beecham Laboratories (major pharmaceutical corp.), Oklahoma City, OK
- Managed annual sales of $6 million; launched two new products.
- Oversaw sales force of ten people covering four states. Recruited, trained, and motivated sales representatives to achieve sales goals.

Sales Representative, (Beecham Laboratories) 1985-89

EDUCATION
B.B.A., University of Missouri, Kansas City, MO 1985

Angela Sinclair
5639 West Northwood Drive, Glendale, Arizona 85041
(602) 939-5532

Job Target: Medical Records Technician

Profile
• More than three years computer and office support experience.
• Highly organized, detail oriented, efficient, and dedicated employee.
• Motivated to learn and grow in responsibility and business skills; work well independently and as a team member.
• Degree in Medical Records Technology.
• Completed 75 hours of directed practice in medical records department at Paradise Valley Hospital.

Employment
Accounting Clerk, 1995-present
Drug Emporium, Corporate Offices, Scottsdale, Arizona
• Performed general accounting duties and data entry.
• Prepared reports with Lotus 1-2-3.
• Handled cash deposits daily and answered phones.

Senior Data Processing Clerk, 1991-1994
AT&T, Mesa, Arizona
• Saved company thousands of dollars each month by investigating high-volume accounts in various computer systems.
• Wrote summations listing problems, resolutions, and revenue saved. Prepared monthly reports listing services worked on and results.
• Dealt with marketing negotiators and engineering personnel to explain problems.
• Investigated, analyzed, and corrected errors for business and residential accounts.

Receptionist and Collections Clerk, 1990-1991
TeleCheck AZ, Inc., Phoenix, Arizona
• Performed daily accounting and banking duties.
• Answered phone, light typing, and filing.

Education
Associate of Applied Science in Medical Records Technology, Phoenix College, 1996. Mesa Community College, 1993, 1992.

Greg Collins
4718 East Desert Lane, Gilbert, Arizona 85062 (602) 807-0696

Objective: Project Management or Field Supervision for Commercial, Industrial, or Public Works projects.

Profile
• Reliable, dependable hands-on manager with ability to get the job done on time and under budget.
• Excel in estimating costs, preparing and maintaining budgets, and purchasing materials.
• Adept in selecting, negotiating and working with contractors to produce quality work consistantly.
• Eight years experience in project management; 18 years experience in working on industrial, commercial, and residential projects.

Professional Experience
Project Manager/Owner (designer and builder of custom homes)
The Collins Group, Gilbert, AZ 1989-present
• Completed nine construction projects ranging from $150,000 to $400,000; all within budget and on time.
• Review bids, hire and supervise specialty subcontractors.
• Draft and maintain budgets, purchase materials.
• Perform 85 percent of construction production with company crew.
• Design and draft building plans including floor plans; mechanical, plumbing, and electrical systems; interior/exterior color coordination and finishes; landscaping.
• Negotiate purchase contracts for land. Market and sell properties after completion.

Contract Negotiator/Construction Coordinator
PF West Inc. (apartment complex developer), Phoenix, AZ 1984-89
• Wrote $60 million in construction contracts without litigation or legal problems. Wrote contracts, pay schedules for each subcontractor.
• Prepared budgets to secure financing; monitored throughout project.
• Selected contractors; maintained progress schedule for each building and overall project.

Education: B.S Construction Management, Arizona State University, Phoenix, AZ 1984. **Current Arizona Licenses:** Master Electrician License, Engineer in Training (E.I.T.), General Building Contractor, Class B, Electrical Contractor, Real Estate Agent

RAYMOND ATKINS
2128 East Kings Avenue, Mesa, Arizona, 85036 • (602) 971-4679

OBJECTIVE: Warehouse Distribution/Management

QUALIFICATIONS
• Over ten years experience in Warehouse Distribution.
• Well versed in ICC Regulations/Rules, International Customs Regulations, Freight Codes, and transportation modes.
• Skilled manager, ability to motivate others, handle conflict effectively.
• Highly organized, challenge-oriented individual.
• Adept in computer entry and shipping/receiving procedures.

EXPERIENCE
Warehouse Layout and Design
• Set up, organized, and maintained off-site Distribution Center.
• Designed floor plan that used space effectively and promoted inventory control. Leased unused space for $500 per month.
• Planned layout of warehouse with limited space to store large loading/unloading trucks and rotating stock.
• Designed stronger, smaller shipping carton resulting in ability to ship larger quantity of product in a single container.

Administration
• Implemented computerized Bills of Lading greatly increasing accuracy.
• Created detailed Logistics Report which resulted in lower shipping rates and better use of regional carriers.

Management
• Effectively handled and resolved conflicts with traffic vendors.
• Supervised nine employees; interviewed, hired and trained new employees; gave ongoing performance reviews.
• Wrote training manual and shipping instructions to save time in training employees and ensure proper procedures were used.

EMPLOYMENT HISTORY
1994-present	Senior Shipping Clerk	Lockheed, Scottsdale, AZ
1990-1994	Material Specialist	Vondavi Tech, Scottsdale, AZ
1986-1990	Warehouse Foreman	American Ind., Scottsdale, AZ

EDUCATION: Paradise Valley Community College, Phoenix, AZ 1995-present. Working toward A.A. Degree in Middle Management.

Daryl Defrancesco
807 East Vista Avenue, Phoenix, AZ 85063 telephone: 602/867-0789

Objective: Data communications, emphasis in customer relations.

Qualifications
- Proficient in training technical, support, and sales personnel.
- Highly successful in developing and maintaining excellent customer relations.
- Goal-oriented professional, committed to a career in data communications.
- Communicate well with international clientele, fluent Spanish.

Experience
Customer Relations
- Principle project manager for two accounts generating $2.5 million in sales, plus eight smaller accounts.
- Provide customer high level of quality service, message integrity, updates on product functionality, and satisfactory answers to technical questions and problems.
- Write software specifications for product development engineers.

Technical Skills
- Troubleshoot problems within the network and during product testing.
- Review software enhancements for customers.
- Install systems in Local Area Networks and dial modes.

Training and Marketing
- Educate salespeople in product knowledge.
- Demonstrate products to prospective customers.
- Train customer's help desk staff in troubleshooting and supporting product.

Employment History
1992-present	*Customer Liaison/Support*	TechNet Systems
1990-92	*Trainer/Customer Service*	TGI Fridays, Inc.
1989-90	*Manager Trainee*	Safeway Corp.

Education
B.A. Business Management, University of Texas, El Paso, TX 1989

Nadine Pike
7501 Sandstone Rd., Tempe, Arizona 85052
(602) 496-3201

Objective: Activities Coordinator for a cruise ship.

Profile
- Outgoing, friendly, people oriented, with a zest for life!
- Skilled in organizing and directing activities with flare.
- Ability to work well with varied personalities in all age groups.
- Flexible: can perform many tasks and learn new skills quickly.
- Athletic, well-groomed, professional appearance.

Experience
Fitness Club Manager and Co-Owner
- Founded two fitness clubs with membership of 400.
- Supervised and trained 14 employees.
- Taught exercise classes and one-on-one personal fitness training.
- Met potential customers to promote fitness programs.
- Performed bookkeeping duties and arranged advertising.

Restaurant-Tavern Manager and Co-Owner
- Business grossed $180,000 annually.
- Designed new menu serving sandwiches, soups, and salads.
- Hired, trained, and supervised employees.
- Maintained accurate inventory, ordered supplies, did bookkeeping.
- Sponsored local baseball teams and participated in activities.

Executive Assistant
- Executive assistant to vice president of a mid-sized tool company.
- Worked on special projects, assisted salespeople, and ordered supplies.

Volunteer Work
- Part-time teacher's assistant for elementary school (seven years).
- Vice President of Parent Teacher Association (one year)
- Camp Fire Leader, Boy Scout Leader (five years)
- Fund-raising for High School Scholarship Program (one year)

Education: Spokane Community College, Spokane, WA (two years)

History of Experience
1991-present	Volunteer leader and worker, parenting
1989-1990	Executive Assistant, Scottsdale Tool Company
1982-1985	Co-owner, Manager, Village Squire Restaurant
1980-1981	Co-owner, Manager, Patricia Hilton Fitness Club

Common Resume Mistakes

- Misspellings, typos, poor grammar
- No objective or too vague
- Exaggeration or too modest
- Too complex, filled with technical jargon
- Not accomplishment oriented
- Too long or too sparse
- Disorganized
- Irrelevant information listed
- Poor appearance
- Type too small
- Narrow margins
- Long blocks of text

Keep These Points in Mind

- Describe your performance, not your responsibilities.
- Stress abilities, skills, and achievements.
- List results and benefits whenever possible.
- Emphasize work history that supports your objective, downplay other work.
- Use a consistent format: matching headings, information shown in consistent way, easy to find information such as dates, titles, education, etc.
- Include studies, seminars, professional affiliations, and volunteer work that *support* your objective.
- Eliminate these words: I..., Responsible for..., Duties include...
- Eliminate personal data such as marital status, children, date of birth, hobbies.
- List education last (usually).
- Do not mention references, salary history, or reasons for leaving any job.
- Use high quality stationery in a light, neutral color.
- Create a resume that is easily read when faxed, copied, or scanned.
- Print your name and phone number on each page in case it gets separated.

- Professionally print your resume or photocopy it NEATLY.
- Envelopes, cover letters, and references should match your resume stationery.
- Never mail or fax your resume without a marketing cover letter.
- Never lie, especially about an educational degree; it is easily verified and will cost you the job, even after being hired.

How to Find a Good Resume Service

Many people have a hard time creating their own effective resume because they are writing about themselves. If you need help, use a good resume service to produce a professional and targeted resume. The service can also help you with cover letters, addressing envelopes, and other job search correspondence.

Try to get a referral from a friend or print shop, or look in the Yellow Pages under "Resume Service." Also try the local newspaper near the want ads or service directory. A good resume writer will ask what your objective is so she can target your resume. The writer will interview you to find out what is unique about you and will learn what skills and accomplishments you have that relate to your objective.

Call at least three to five resume services. Request to speak to the person who will actually write your resume and ask these questions:

What is your technique? Do you write the resume with the job seeker present? (That's the best way.) If I'm not present, how do you get the right information? How long is the interview?

How do you plan to overcome my special obstacle? (Everyone has one—career change, work gaps, inexperience, overqualified, too many jobs, too old or too young, etc.)

How would you handle several job targets? (if that's your situation)

What exactly is included in the price? How many copies? A computer disc? Revisions? Cover letter? List of references? Changes? Updates?

What makes your resumes better than anyone else's?

Do you write targeted cover letters?

What is the cost? Get an estimate even if it's an amount per hour and the time varies. As usual, you get what you pay for—a good resume can range between $75 and $300. Avoid the "cheapies." Services that won't tell you the price over the phone are usually very high and are counting on hard selling you when you arrive.

When you meet with the writer, before you commit your money, look at written samples to make sure that writer meets your expectations.

A good resume service can be an asset to your job search. A bad resume service will be a detriment. Choose carefully.

PART II

Market Yourself to Success

Marketing Strategies

The vast majority of the job market is not found in want ads or employment agencies. Recent surveys from employers show as many as 80 to 90 percent of all job openings are not advertised. How are these positions filled? Let's look at the steps that take place before a job is advertised.

Four Stages of a Job Opening

Stage One	Stage Two	Stage Three	Stage Four
No job opening, but employers are always looking for good workers.	The need is clear, the insiders know, but no action is taken.	Job now "open." Referrals desired, applications being accepted.	Ad is in the paper. The thundering horde appears.

From *The Very Quick Job Search*, by J. Michael Farr. Copyright 1991, 1996, used with permission

About **half** of those hired make the initial employer contact during the first two stages. There are many reasons why this works. Good employers know they will always have turnover and keep an eye out for good employees. Employers also create new jobs, may be unhappy with an employee's performance, know an employee is leaving soon, or have plans for expansion—all before a job is officially open. A worker may also give his notice unexpectedly. Introducing yourself to the employer during these first two stages gives you a decided edge—plus the competition is virtually eliminated.

When the job becomes officially "open" (stage three), the employer's first choice is to hire someone she has already met or who is referred by someone she knows. For the employer, hiring a qualified person without having to advertise is infinitely easier, faster, and less expensive. Another 25 percent of people hired make the first contact in stage three by asking if there is a job opening and applying to the company directly. This works, but the job seeker is still missing 50 percent of the jobs available from the first two stages.

As a result, most quality jobs are filled long before they reach stage four—advertising. *The jobs that end up in the want ads tend to be undesirable or harder to fill.* And if that weren't enough, in stage four you're competing with galloping herds of rivals. Yet, many people conduct their job search primarily in one way: using the want ads. It's no wonder they despair.

The "hidden job market" simply means unadvertised job openings. The *whopping majority of jobs found are unadvertised (80 to 90 percent).*

Strategy: Don't wait for job openings, look for potential openings.

In order to find potential openings and market yourself most effectively, you need to know which job search methods work best. Let's look at the most *unsuccessful* methods first.

Most Unsuccessful Job Search Methods

- Using computer listings or registers
- Answering local newspaper ads
- Going to private employment agencies
- Answering ads in professional or trade journals
- Mass mailing of resumes

Note that the most *unsuccessful* job search methods are used after the job is advertised (stage four) and they go through a third party such as the computer, newspaper or magazine, or an employment agency. These methods, and mass mailing resumes, are highly impersonal plus putting you smack dab in the middle of hundreds of competing rivals, hence their downfall. However, if you are searching for a job in the computer industry, it makes sense to list your resume in a computer bank. Or if you want to cover all the bases, that's fine. Just be sure to use the most *successful* job search methods also.

Now let's take a look at the most *successful* ways to find a job.

Most Successful Job Search Methods

- The creative job-hunting approach
- Applying directly to an employer, factory, or office in person
- Asking friends and acquaintances for job leads
- Asking relatives for job leads
- Using the placement office at the school, college you attended

The number one most successful method is **the creative job-hunting approach.** In *What Color Is Your Parachute?*, Richard Bolles describes it as "...figuring out your best skills, and favorite knowledges, and then researching any employer that interests you, before approaching that organization and arranging, through your contacts, to see the person there who has the power to hire you for the position you are interested in. This method, faithfully followed, leads to a job for 86 out of every 100 job-hunters who try it."

If you have completed Appendix A and/or Part I, you have already identified your top skills, knowledges, and favorite industries as described in the creative job-hunting method. You have defined your job target. The next steps are to market yourself, primarily using the top methods—networking and approaching employers directly. And of course, you'll want to make the best approach to employers using information you have uncovered in research.

Doesn't it make sense to target unadvertised jobs using the most successful job search techniques?

Even though it makes sense, you still want to make sure you're not skipping anything. The answer is to spend your time proportionately on each method.

Most Effective Job Search Time Management

- 80-90 percent of job search time spent defining your job target, networking, and approaching employers directly
- 5-10 percent of job search time answering want ads
- 5-10 percent of job search time with executive recruiters, employment agencies, job marts, computer listings, etc.
- Spend a minimum of 40 hours per week on your job search, 20 hours if you're currently working

Looking for a job is a job. Get up every morning, and shower and dress as if you were going to work. Plan your day and your week, making goals for each week. Schedule blocks of time for specific activities: want ads on Sunday morning until noon; agencies on Monday morning; and the rest of the week creative job-hunting method, networking, and applying directly to employers. Write letters and make calls in the mornings, go out and see people every afternoon. Spend your entire days and entire weeks doing job search activities and read job search materials in the evening. Even if you have a job now, the same principles apply: spend a minimum of 20 hours per week on your job search.

Your reward is equal to your efforts.

The most important marketing strategy is networking—to get many eyes and ears in the job market working for you to uncover job leads. One person simply cannot do it. Networking also produces valuable information about companies you want to work for and the qualifications they prefer. And best of all, networking develops important contacts to help you set up interviews.

Networking is telling everyone you know, and new people you meet, that you are in the job market and what type of work you're looking for.

When networking, it's crucial that you communicate what you want to do. People can't help you unless they know what you want.

You may think you don't know the right people who have contacts that can help you, but you are wrong. It's been proven time and time again that we're all seemingly connected by a huge net, hence the term "networking." Consider the following true stories.

In one of my seminars we were practicing networking using a 30-second commercial. After the exercise, one man turned to another and said, "I overheard that you wanted to work at ABC Corporation. My neighbor hires for the position you're targeting. I'll introduce you."

A technical writer had been laid off and unable to find a permanent job in his field for several years. One day, his father was chatting with the tree-trimmer he had hired and discovered that the tree-trimmer's wife was the department head of a technical writers group and was looking for a writer. He told the tree-trimmer of his son, and the son was hired within the month.

A career counselor was working with a woman who was extremely shy and couldn't bring herself to tell anyone that she was looking for a job. The counselor finally convinced her to call at least one person—her brother. Her brother lived two states away, but when he learned what type of work she was looking for he referred her to a friend in her city who helped her land a good job.

In a scriptwriting class the instructor told us the only way to get your screenplay read by someone in Hollywood is through a contact. He said, "I bet everyone in this room knows someone who knows someone in Hollywood." I thought that theory was stretching it since my lifestyle is about the farthest from Hollywood that you can get. But later that same week in a writers group, I discovered a fellow group member's cousin is the actor, Jonathan Frakes, who played Lt. Riker on *Star Trek*.

At a seminar I attended, the speaker was addressing networking and mentioned the phenomenon that each of us is only seven people away from any person in the United States. He informed us that he personally was only two people away from the president of the United States. He paused and a man from the front row said, "Then I am only three people away from the president."

Networking works.

Turn Leads Into Interviews

Did you know that more than two-thirds of all jobs openings are in small businesses with fewer than twenty-five employees? You'll find a job much faster by targeting this lucrative market. Small companies are also the easiest to approach.

The most effective ways to arrange a meeting or interview with prospective employers are:
- Using your contacts.
- Applying directly to the company in person.
- Using a combination of methods: making an appointment by phone, sending a marketing letter and resume followed by phone calls, using information from networking and research in your approach, and having a systematic method for your entire job search.

Your preparation pays off now. Use the valuable information you have assembled—your top skills, the employers' needs, contacts, and company research—in your presentations to set up a meeting. Above all, be politely persistent, and follow through diligently.

Once you hear about a job opening, a possible opportunity, or a company you would like to work for, find out the exact name of the hiring person. This person would probably be your boss if you were hired: a department head, vice president, or CEO in a large company or the owner or manager in a small company. You can learn the person's name by asking your contacts, through research at the library (both always verified by calling the company), and calling the company and asking the receptionist the name and spelling of the owner, department head, manager, or VP you are targeting.

Do not go through the personnel or human resource (HR) office. The HR office usually doesn't know about a job opening until Stage Four and its primary purpose is to screen people out. Besides, the majority of jobs are with smaller companies, which don't have human resource departments.

Next, arrange a meeting with the hiring person or decision maker. You can do this in a number of ways; 1) through your contacts, 2) call the hiring person directly, 3) write to them and follow up with a phone call, 4) visit them in person, or 5) use a combination of these methods. Be politely persistent until you have set up a meeting.

Have you ever noticed how the proper tool makes a task so much easier? It's the same in your job search. Each tool is designed for a specific task, but you must take the initiative to create the tools and use them. You have already created one valuable tool—a targeted resume. In this section we will discuss more useful tools and how to use them to market yourself successfully. Them we'll take a detailed look at the most effective techniques to help turn leads into appointments: using your contacts, applying in person, using the telephone, using a targeted cover letter. Each strategy will use a combination of techniques.

STEP 4

Design a Networking Card

A small card to hand out is extremely helpful when you're meeting people, networking, or sending letters and cards by mail. Your resume is too large and detailed for this project, but a small card is easy to carry in your pocket or purse and easy for the recipient to keep. A personal networking card will help people remember you, and it is invaluable in helping them to pass your name to others.

Choose a size that works best for you—a business card (3.5 x 2) or a 5 x 3 card. At the top, state your name, phone number(s), and objective. The objective, or job target, is important because that's how people know you're looking for a job. Remember, this isn't a normal business card. Choose a few of the best highlights from your resume—qualifications taken from your profile and/or one or two achievements. This card is intended to get people to remember you and call you. Don't pack the space with text— make it easy to read.

Have these cards printed by a desktop publisher, a resume service, or your local copy/print shop. Examples:

Ashley Stevens   (602) 992-2020
Career objective: Teacher, grades K to 8th
- Excel in using creative, alternative teaching methods
- Ability to make learning a pleasure rather than a duty
- Five years teaching experience, BA Liberal Arts
- Dedicated to teaching and working with children
- Enthusiastic, responsible, and mature

JOHN KILMER, seeking a position in
Hotel, Restaurant, and Nightclub Management
602.483.7072 • pager 602.578.9876

• Keen ability to develop profitable business
  ventures
• Increased one restaurant's annual revenue from
  $500,000 to $2.6 million
• Over ten years experience directing successful
  high-volume hotels, restaurants, and nightclubs

Keep your networking cards with you at all times, and hand them out to everyone you meet. Give them to your friends and relatives to hand out. Mail one or two with every letter, thank-you note, and resume you send out. These cards really work, because they're easy to give and easy to keep. Make them interesting to read while getting your point across, and it will be easy for people to call you with job leads.

STEP 5

Create a 30-second Commercial

Before you begin networking, it's wise to prepare a 30-second "commercial" about the work you want to do next. People are more willing and able to help if they understand what you want to do and you can communicate it with confidence. Begin your commercial with your objective as described by function and industry in your resume, then add a few qualifications taken from the profile in your resume. For a personal touch, you might add why you want to do this type of work (your beliefs and values). Think of it as your oral networking card.

A sample commercial sounds like this:

> *"Hello! My name is Ashley Stevens. I'm in the job market, and I'm interested in a teaching position in grades kindergarten to eighth grade. My special skills are using alternative teaching methods and arts and crafts. I'm deeply committed to helping each child develop his or her highest potential."*

This commercial works because it's descriptive and to the point. The last thing you want to do is bore the listener with a bunch of vague statements or drone on... and on... and on. It's easy to inject natural confidence and energy into your commercial because *this is who you are.* You've done your homework, so you're speaking from facts, from a solid foundation. People are naturally interested and want to help such a positive, upbeat person who knows where he or she is going.

It's important to put this script in your own words and to practice it out loud until it becomes second nature to you. Use the following script to get started.

"Hello! My name is _____, and I'm looking for a job as a _____ . My skills/accomplishments/qualifications are _____, _____, and _____. I want to do this type of work because _____. Do you know anyone in this line of work?"

Now you have two valuable tools to begin networking—your networking card and your networking script. Let's build your network beginning with some very important people—your references.

STEP 6

Enlist Your References

Your references play two important roles in your job search: 1) to verify your past work, accomplishments, and skills to potential employers and 2) to serve as a source for job leads.

More than ever, a personal testimonial is important to confirm the positive impression you worked so hard to achieve in the interview. Today, many companies do not give out employment verification other than names and dates, because of the growing number of lawsuits. It's frustrating and difficult for the employer performing a background check to speak to your previous boss because of the barrage of obstacles: company switchboards, electronic telephone services, and finding the correct location to call. And what if your previous boss was transferred, promoted, changed jobs, or moved?

Usually the prospective employer is referred back to the human resource department and can only verify name, rank, and dates. What they really want to know is your former boss's opinion of your work performance and ethics. The answers to those questions and other spontaneous comments can only come from a personal conversation. Businesses also perform background checks for employers.

Of course, you will screen your references first so you *know* they'll give you an excellent recommendation and are standing by to do so. Questions you can expect a potential employer to ask your reference include:
- Is she eligible for rehire?
- Why did she leave?
- What were her duties, and how did she perform them?
- How did she work with peers, management, or employees?

- What characteristics would you say best describe her?
- Were there any problems with her performance?
- Would you verify her employment title, dates, and salary?

Many employers will not verify salary, but some do—don't lie about it.

Make it easy for your interviewer by providing a complete list of references—you'll appear professional and prepared. The appropriate time to hand out your list of references is immediately after an interview you feel good about. Employers are not interested in your references until they have a strong interest in hiring you, nor do they have time to wade through extra pages when first reviewing your resume. Providing references at the close of a successful interview will also prevent them from being bothered needlessly.

A letter of reference doesn't work very well because it is often drafted by the employee himself, or doesn't address what the prospective employer wants to know, or it can't be verified. If it's impossible for the prospective employer to call your reference (he moved to Africa), then a letter will help, but it usually won't have much influence. An exception would be from a highly prestigious person that's hard to reach by phone.

References are a strategic job lead source if they are treated considerately and wisely. Your references know you well, both professionally and personally, are probably in a segment of the job market you are targeting, and have many contacts. They are additional "eyes and ears" for you in the job market: They can keep you informed of new opportunities (job leads), can tell you of new developments in your field (more job leads), and are in a perfect position to recommend you.

I worked with a woman who had relocated across the country, wasn't sure what she wanted to do, and took the first job she could find. Six months later she was miserable. Her job became unbearable, and after reassessing her situation, she decided to get back into her previous career—retail management. She called her old boss (whom she hadn't talked with for three years) told him of her plans, and asked him if he'd be her reference. He was excited—his retail chain was currently in negotiations to buy three stores in her city, and he wanted her to oversee them. He offered her the position over the phone, and she was elated. Before she called him, she had not known of the expansion, and he had not known of her move.

Create a powerful Reference List and begin networking by following these guidelines:

1. Identify your references.

The best references are former supervisors familiar with your work. Other good references are prestigious people in your targeted field and prestigious people the prospective employer would recognize or who would elevate your status in some way. Alternatives might be teachers and professors, co-workers, vendors, customers, and clients. Personal references that don't fit any of the above categories have little influence but are better than none.

2. Talk to them.

Call or visit each potential reference, describe the kind of work you wish to do, and ask if they will be your reference. Tell them you will give out their number only to serious prospective employers so they won't be bothered by unnecessary calls. Most people are glad to help and are flattered by your request. If you sense hesitation on the part of your reference, or think there may be a problem, get it out in the open and resolve it. It's better to find out now than to lose potential jobs over it. If it's not possible to reconcile, drop that person as a reference. NEVER ask your references for a job, but do ask them to let you know of new developments, opportunities, and job leads in your field. If they have a job for you, they will volunteer it.

3. Prepare your Reference List.

On a separate page of stationery that matches your resume, use the same heading as your resume with your name, address, and phone number. Skip down a few lines and type "References" and list them like this:

Direct supervisor: Jeanette Murphy, VP Marketing
Acme Company, Inc.
1234 N. Main Street, Suite 202

Phoenix, AZ 85028
(602) 966-4949, ext. 3201

List the relationship to you and use complete titles, business addresses, phone numbers, and extensions to make it easy for the prospective employer. You may also use Ms. or Mr. for a more formal approach or to designate male or female gender for names like Pat, Terry, and Chris.

Use current titles and company names. If your reference's title or company has changed since she was your boss, list it as shown below so the new employer will know who did what and which questions to ask.

Direct supervisor: Jeanette Murphy, VP Sales and Marketing
(formerly Western Division Sales Manager)

———

Direct supervisor: Jeanette Murphy, VP Marketing
Acme Company, Inc.
(formerly Public Relations Officer of XYZ Corporation)

4. Write to them.

After they have agreed to be one of your references, send them two copies of your resume, a typed letter of thanks, and a few networking cards. In the letter, reiterate the kind of work you are seeking, and ask them to let you know of any opportunities or information that may help you in your job search. Your resume helps refresh their memory of dates and accomplishments as well as the direction in which you're headed.

5. Keep in touch.

Call them every one or two weeks regarding calls they can expect from prospective employers. Encourage them to share the conversation from background checks with you—it provides excellent feedback. Don't forget to ask if they know of any new job leads.

STEP 7

Build Your Network

Your goals in networking are to:
• let people know you're in the job market and what work you're targeting
• get as many people as possible looking for job leads for you
• uncover unadvertised job leads
• open more lines of communication
• increase your knowledge of specific businesses and industries
• practice your interviewing skills
• set up meetings and interviews

Networking is the number one way to find a good job, especially when combined with the targeted job approach. Yet many people underrate this step because they are embarrassed to be in the job market or they think they are too shy to talk to people. Well, get over it! Today, almost everyone has been in the job market—it doesn't have the negative stigma it had twenty years ago. Look at this as a great opportunity to improve your lifestyle and find an exciting, fulfilling job. Your networking contacts will want to help you, particularly if you maintain a focused, positive attitude.

The people you talk to, or network with, are your relatives, friends, neighbors, social acquaintances, co-workers, former co-workers, bosses, classmates, teachers, and members from clubs, associations, and your church. A good place to start is your address book and Christmas/holiday card list. Don't overlook your contacts in the service industries: your hair stylist, lawyer, bank teller, accountant, insurance agent, doctor, or anyone you meet.

Take out a clean sheet of paper to keep a record of your contacts. List your references first because you've already networked with them. Next, write down your relatives and close friends, then as many names as you can think of.

Set aside some uninterrupted time every day to *call every person* on your list. Begin with your 30-second commercial. If the person you're talking with is interested, then elaborate more on your qualifications and the type of work you are seeking, but keep it brief. Treat each networking contact as a mentor or advisor. Do not ask your contacts for a job—this puts them on the defensive. If they know of a job in their company, they will volunteer it—if they think you're qualified. (If your contact is a hiring authority, your approach will be different as explained later.) Ask questions that lead to job information and job leads. Be frank—show that you're committed and mean business. Here are some sample questions to ask after you've shared your commercial.

Networking Questions
- Do you know of any information that may help my job search?
- Do you know of any job leads or potential opportunities in my field?
- Do you know anyone who does the kind of work I want to do?
- Do you know the names of companies that do this kind of work?
- Do you know anyone who works at companies that do this kind of work?
- What are the names and phone numbers of these people, and may I use your name when I talk to them?

Try to get two or more referrals from each person you talk with. In this manner, your network will grow and grow.

Once you find contacts who are in the same line of work that you want to be in or work in a company you're interested in, then make appointments with these people. Call them and use the name of the person who referred you, give your 30-second commercial, and ask to meet with them for twenty minutes to learn more about their work or company. Respect each person's time, and stick to your schedule.

Try these additional networking questions when you are talking face-to-face with someone doing the kind of work you want or working in a company you're interested in:
- How did you get your job?
- How did you break into this field?
- What do you like most/least about your job?
- What is your greatest challenge?
- What is your company like? (philosophy, working conditions, structure)
- What professional publications in this industry should I read?
- What are the associations and organizations associated with this industry?
- Who are the recognized leaders in this field?
- What's a typical career path for someone coming in at my level?
- Do you think my skills/experience/knowledge would benefit the company?
- Is there formal or on-the-job training?
- Which other professionals should I contact?
- What is the name of the person who hires for this position?
- May I use your name when I talk to him?
- Would you mind calling him in advance so he knows who I am when I call?

Call your best contacts regularly (every one or two weeks), but have a reason to call them—new developments, interesting industry tidbits, or people they may want to meet. Call the "cold" contacts (least helpful) when things are slow—they could change suddenly from a cold lead to a hot one.

Be sure to attend trade and professional association meetings, club meetings, networking groups, breakfasts, seminars, and social gatherings—anywhere there is an opportunity to meet people. With each contact, exchange information and business cards. **ALWAYS** carry your networking cards with you and a few copies of your resume. By attending meetings and social gatherings you will constantly be replenished with new contacts.

Remember that networking is about developing professional relationships—not a game to see how many cards you can hand out. Throughout your job search continue networking no matter how promising your interviews or job offers are. Networking is a life skill that your career is increasingly dependent upon no matter where you are working or the level of your career.

If you come to a lull and run out of contacts, go back over your networking list and touch base with people you haven't talked to for at least two or three weeks. Call your cold leads for new developments, look for new meetings to attend, ask your contacts for referrals.

Of course, the ultimate goal of networking is to get interviews with the decision makers—the people who have the authority to hire you.

STEP 8

Thank Them with a Note

Buy a supply of tasteful thank-you cards. *Every night,* hand-write a thank-you note to each person who helped you or you networked with that day, and enclose your networking card. Especially include receptionists and assistants. This helps them to remember you and think of you in very good terms. These are the very people you may be calling later to help you set up an interview or provide more information and leads. You never know from which direction THE job lead will come.

Sample hand-written thank-you notes:

Dear Cindy,
    Thank you for referring me to Mr. Crumble at Coco's Cookie Factory and calling him personally to set up our meeting on Thursday.
    Your help is greatly appreciated!

                        Sincerely,
                        Louis Clark

Dear Jack,
    I enjoyed meeting you at the Chamber of Commerce breakfast this morning. I am especially interested in your new company, Fast Tracks, and will pass on your name to Bob Williams at BBI as we discussed.
    Thanks for the two names you gave me to aid in my job search as a programer—I'm sure they will be helpful.

                    Gary Winslow

These notes are used to express your gratitude for someone's help and are hand-written because it is proper good manners to do so. They also happen to be beneficial in your job search. Please do not confuse these casual thank-you notes with a formal thank-you business letter sent after a job interview that is typed or printed in business letter style and outlines why the company should hire you. (See Step 18, Follow-up with Proven Strategies.)

STEP 9

Develop Prospective Employer Files

What are the names of the companies that perform the type of work you want to do? This information comes from networking and research. Both are essential to your job search. You probably know a few names of companies through advertising or simply the reputation of the company. Begin a Prospective Employer Action File using these names, and add more from your networking contacts.

The best way to track your progress and have the company information at your fingertips is to use 5 x 7-inch cards with a card file. This is your Prospective Employer Action File. Record the company's name, address, phone number, and more information as you gather it, such as the name of the hiring authority, and dates, names, and actions of your contacts with the company. Use one card for each company and divide the prospective employers into three sections: Hot, Warm, and Cold. Naturally, the prospects in your Hot file are your best leads and the ideal companies for which you want to work. Good possibilities go in the Warm file. The Cold file is for prospects about which you're doubtful or need to find out more information. Or perhaps you've tried everything else (networking, contacts, walk-in, letters, phone calls), and you can't get a meeting set up—but that could change. It's just cold *right now*. Here's an example of Prospective Employer Action File.

Company: Acme Widgets, Inc.

Phone: 484-9402

Contact: Angela Smith, Sales & Marketing Dept. Head

Address: 1104 Balboa Blvd, Granada Hills, CA 91344

4/2 Angela on vacation, back 4/7

4/7 Can't get through, no message

4/8 Talked to Angela, said to send resume, sent today w/cover letter

4/10 Left message

4/11 Out of office today, left message

4/14 Called Angela, set up meeting for 4/15

4/15 Interview went well, sent thank-you letter

4/17 Called Angela, said Terry Brown makes final decision next week. Set 2nd meeting for 4/21 with Terry Brown, I am one of three candidates.

4/21 Had good meeting & company tour, decision will be made by 4/23

4/22 Hand delivered thank-you letter to TB, talked to Angela

4/23 a.m. Called Terry, repeated why the company would benefit from hiring me, why I want to work there

4/24 Job offer!

Have you ever wanted to be a detective? Now is a good time to start. Add names of companies to your Prospective Employer Action File by looking through the Yellow Pages under the industries you are targeting. Get a list of business members from trade or professional associations. Read the local daily and business newspapers—they can provide current information to use in your communications as well as job and company leads. Which companies are expanding? Moving to your city? Introducing new products? Starting up? Who's getting promoted? Pay particular attention to smaller, privately held companies because that's where the most jobs are.

Next, visit the reference section of a large library (the largest in your city) for more leads and information on companies. Ask the reference librarian for help in locating the appropriate directories targeting your specific field and geographical area. Or you can start with a general directory such as the *Guide to American Directories* and *Directories in Print.* Refer to Appendix B for a comprehensive list of sources.

For the Hot and Warm prospective employers, you want to gather as much information as possible. The more knowledgeable you are, the greater the chances of finding a company that's right for you and of landing the job. For larger, public companies, you'll find financial information reported to their stockholders. Smaller companies may be harder to find, but try the local newspapers and magazines. Ask the reference librarian for help and ideas.

Keep accurate records of information you gather: make photocopies, hand write, or print out the information from the library. Make a separate Employer Information File and use 8.5 x 11-inch manila folders to store this information alphabetically by company. The 5 x 7-inch cards are your Action Files, while the manila folders are your Information Files that contain articles, brochures, data, and facts about your prospective employers. This information will help you decide if you want to work there and to tailor your approach to the company. When you are invited for a sudden interview or called for a "telephone interview," these files and their pertinent information will be at your fingertips.

Use your research in conjunction with networking. Ask people about companies you've uncovered, and research companies you've learned about through networking. Facts on either side are not always 100 percent accurate.

You'll start out with an abundance of prospective employers. Through your research and talking with people, you can eliminate the employers that don't match your standards. You'll get better results targeting twelve well-researched companies rather than fifty vague names on a list.

Every Monday morning (or Sunday evening) review your Hot and Warm files, and plan your week for phone calls, letters, meetings, and interviews. Through your contacts, try to meet with anyone who works in the target company—they can provide invaluable information for an upcoming interview.

When things are slow, review your cold files to determine if there are any changes and what your action should be. A lead is never dead. Even if the company closed, the people still went somewhere. If a month has passed after your initial contact without any positive response from the company, start over as if you had never contacted them before. Situations can change rapidly, and this technique works fifty percent of the time.

STEP 10

Arrange Interviews Through Your Contacts

Obviously, the most desired situation is if your contact calls in advance for you and arranges a meeting or introduction with the decision maker. That is why you work so diligently to build your network! The employer considers these referrals seriously because people usually don't recommend a person for a job unless he or she is qualified. When a person helps a boss, co-worker, or friend to solve a major problem such as hiring a good candidate for a job, it makes them look good and puts them in a position of being owed a favor. People *like* to refer qualified people for jobs. On the other hand, if they have any doubts, they won't refer you, because it reflects badly on them.

If you have built your network, as outlined in the networking section, you have a core of contacts to help you make appointments for interviews. Now is the time to call back the acquaintances you have met, kept in touch with, and sent thank-you notes to. Your goal is to get a referral from your contact directly to a decision maker and/or have the contact call to make an appointment or introduction with the decision maker.

A sample telephone call:

"Hi, Charlie, this is Vicki Stromburg. We met last week at the NetCom Breakfast. I've decided to apply to XYZ Company as a programmer. I know you do a lot of business with them. Do you know anyone in the software group?"

"Actually, I know a couple of people over there. Alan King and Jon Conifer. Jon would be the one you'd want to talk with, but I don't think they're hiring."

> *"It doesn't matter if they are hiring right now, I just want a chance to talk with him. Would you mind if I used your name when I talk to him, or would you mind talking with him so he knows who I am when I call?"*
>
> *"No, not at all. In fact, I'll call him now and tell him to expect your call."*
>
> *"Thanks, I really appreciate it!"*

Keep in mind that Vicki has done her background work. At the breakfast, she recited her commercial, so Charlie knows what she's looking for and why she's qualified. He made a few suggestions for her job search, and she obtained his business card and gave him her networking card. She also mailed him a thank-you note for the suggestions and mentioned how they worked for her. He knows she's professional and qualified for the work she's seeking, so he's happy to refer her. He just wishes he had thought of it first.

The second best alternative is for Vicki to make the phone call herself and mention that Charlie referred her. This works well, too. Ask your contacts face-to-face or on the telephone for their help. Letters don't work as well. If your contact works in the company you want to apply to, try this:

> *"Hi, Ron. This is Vicki Sromburg. We met at Marilyn's barbecue last Saturday."*
>
> *"Yes, Vicki. Have you dried off from the rain?"*
>
> *"Oh, a little rain never hurt anyone! I'm calling because I'm very interested in working in the art department in your company, XYZ, as we had discussed. You mentioned that Louanne Riseling runs the show, and I'd like to set up a meeting with her. Would you mind if I used your name when I call her?"*
>
> *"Please do. If fact, I had mentioned you may be contacting her."*
>
> *"Thanks, Ron!"*

Please remember that networking is about building relationships. Your contacts must trust you in order for them to refer you personally.

STEP 11

Apply in Person

Applying in person works well with small companies regardless of the level of position. Ask for the decision maker by name, since you have called in advance for this information. If he or she cannot see you at that time, make an appointment. Use your 30-second commercial to explain the reason. You want an appointment regardless of whether there are any openings. If all else fails, fill out an application or leave your resume, then make a follow-up phone call the next day, and the next day...

I know one man who found a job by visiting the city he wanted to move to. He drove around downtown until he saw a large, impressive building that housed a title company, his targeted industry. He walked in and asked to chat with a vice president and was granted an audience. He hit it off with the VP, was given a tour of the company and offered a job, which he started within two weeks.

In another instance, a woman who had just obtained her real estate license, but had no experience, wanted to work for new home builder. She targeted the top ten builders in her city and visited subdivisions from each one. On her one day off per week from her current job, she visited the corporate offices of each builder and asked for the VP of Sales by name. If they couldn't meet with her, she left a targeted cover letter and resume she had prepared in advance. She gained two impromptu meetings with VPs and was hired by the second one.

Another man wanted to be an auto repair shop manager for a large car dealer. He was visiting a prospective car dealer and overheard two salespeople talking about the sloppy work performance and poor management of the body shop. He promptly sent his resume and targeted cover letter to the General Manager, was invited for several interviews, and hired.

A woman had just completed school for interior design, and her only experience was an internship. At lunch time, she entered the company she was targeting with her portfolio in hand. She walked up to the man who was searching for something behind the receptionist's desk. She began talking to him using her 30-second commercial. She asked if there was anyone available she could meet with.

The man said, "Yes, how about me? I'm the president, and I rarely have a chance to talk to new people. Come into the conference room, and show me your portfolio." She was hired by the president.

Initiative works.

STEP 12

Make Appointments by Telephone

Making an appointment by phone can work, too. Call your targeted company, and ask for the person who would hire you. If you don't know, ask for the name of the department head, manager, CEO, foreman, or supervisor of your targeted position, then have the call put through. Be sure to get the person's name (and spelling), so you can follow up later. It may be difficult to get through to some people, and we'll discuss that later in this section.

What do you say when you get the decision maker on the line? Use your 30-second commercial to begin your script, and close it by asking for a meeting. Expect people to say no, or more likely, "We aren't hiring." Your goal is to get a meeting regardless of whether they have an opening or are accepting applications. As you know, they may not be hiring right now, *but a position could open or be created at any time.* And you want them to think of you first.

Try this script, then develop one of your own:

Hello, Mr./Ms. _____. My name is _____. I was referred by _____. I'm a _____ and my skills (and/or accomplishments) are _____, _____, and _____. I'm interested in _____. I want to meet with you to discuss employment opportunities. When would be a good time for you?

Telephone script examples

"Hello, Ms. Simon, my name is Sandra Miller. Jim Mattson from the Telecom Group suggested I call you. I'm interested in a position in your marketing department. I have five years experience in successfully launch-

ing new products—very similar to your new line of wid-
gets. I would like to meet with you briefly. When would
be a good time for you?"

If you have the name of a referral, always use it as soon as possible. Even if you were referred by the CEO's assistant to a department head, it's still a referral.

Use information about their company to show you're knowledgeable about their business, or have at least taken the initiative to do some research. The more you know about them, the more clout you have, which increases your chances of a meeting.

> *"Hello, Mr. Clark. My name is Joe Phillips. I'm in-*
> *terested in a position as an electrician. I've worked for*
> *several major home builders in this area. I'm reliable,*
> *hard-working, and take pride in doing my job right the*
> *first time. I'd like to meet with you in the next day or*
> *two if possible. When would be a good time for you?"*
> *"We don't have any jobs open right now."*
> *"I understand. I still would like to meet with you in*
> *case anything opens up in the near future. You never know*
> *when that could happen. And when it does, you'll want a*
> *reliable, experienced electrician. Would tomorrow morn-*
> *ing or afternoon be better for you?"*
> *"I really don't plan on hiring for the next six months*
> *or so."*
> *"Then I'd like to talk to you about what you do.*
> *Your company ranks in the top three in this city, and I'm*
> *interested in knowing more so I can find a position and*
> *move up. Perhaps you can advise me. All I ask is fifteen*
> *minutes or less of your time. What do you say?"*

If you still get a no after trying several times, ask if they know of anyone else you could contact. Often they will have friends in the same or similar business and can refer you. They are still a prospective employer. If they referred you to someone, send them a thank-you note with your networking card. If not, send them a letter and networking card, or letter and resume. Call them again in about three or four weeks. Your name will start to be familiar to them. If you check with their receptionist or assistant every week, you'll gain a reputation as being persistent, a go-getter (as long as you're always polite and friendly). That's a trait that any employer would want in an employee.

It's very important to write your script the way you talk, so it will sound natural. After writing it out and practicing, just jot down the main points you want to make, so you will speak naturally. Practice your script out loud until you feel comfortable and confident. Call a friend and practice over the phone.

If you have trouble getting through to the decision maker try these methods:

- Mention the name of your referral.
- Call before or after business hours or during lunch.
- Get referred from a higher office such as the president's personal assistant.
- Mail a letter/resume stating you will call at a specific time or date, then your call is expected.
- Ask what time they will be available, then call back.
- Make an appointment to call back at a convenient time.
- Call with confidence, asking for the person by first name, as if you were a personal friend.
- Ask the secretary or assistant for help.
- If nothing else works, leave a message on voice mail, using your 30-second commercial.

Try several times to reach the person without leaving a message. If that doesn't work, then leave a message mentioning your referral, if you have one. Try to avoid saying you are looking for a job. Instead give a valid reason for a meeting—you want to discuss ideas about a specific item or task. After the first few times, always leave a message, and call back once every day for ten days before abandoning a lead. Try sending a letter through the mail, too.

Remember Charlie Sheen in the movie *Wall Street?* He played a stockbroker and was trying to get in to see the biggest hot shot of all, Gordon Gekko, played by Michael Douglas. He called *every day for 54 days* and was on a first name basis with the secretary. Then he walked in with a birthday gift for Mr. Gekko (information he uncovered by research) and asked if he could see him that day. The answer was yes, for a few minutes. And then...finally the doors were opened! He was admitted to the inner circle. Gordon Gekko immediately said, "What do you know that I don't already know? Come on, you only have a few minutes."

This scene is very much like getting an interview or meeting set up and then being able to show the employer why he should hire you instead of someone else. Hopefully, you won't have to go through this much effort to gain a meeting, but wouldn't it be worth it to have an opportunity to work with the very top dog in your field?

STEP 13

Market Your Talents with a Cover Letter

Sometimes you have to mail a resume and/or a letter to an employer. The letter sent with a resume is commonly known as a cover letter. Instead, think of it as a marketing letter. The marketing letter is an important opportunity to market your skills and expertise to a specific decision maker at a targeted company. It may be your only chance to open the door. A marketing letter may be used without a resume, but a resume should **always** be accompanied by a personalized marketing letter when mailed or faxed.

The most powerful marketing letters grab employer's attention from the first line and makes them sit up and take notice, then reach for the phone to call you. How? The marketing letter is targeted to a specific company and decision maker you've gleaned information about from networking and research. Your letter demonstrates your knowledge about the company's problems/challenges/goals and what benefits you bring to the table. It closes with action for the next step. If your letter is received before the company advertises for the position, you eliminate 90 to 95 percent of your competition. Consider these true stories.

Jessie mass mailed 300 generic cover letters and resumes, was invited to four interviews that resulted in one mediocre job offer.

Julie thoroughly researched companies she wanted to work for and sent out fifteen well-written marketing letters and resumes. She was invited to six interviews resulting in three job offers. One was outstanding, and she accepted. After she started her new job, her boss revealed that *her* boss had given her the letter and said, "If you don't hire this woman, you're crazy."

Another woman targeted six companies for a sales position and mailed personalized marketing letters and resumes to each one. Immediately upon receiving her letter, one VP called her and said, "I just read your letter and would feel like an idiot if I didn't interview you. I don't have any openings right now, but I'd like to meet you."

Your marketing letter should:
- be individually written to each company
- mention the company name once or twice in the body of the letter
- be addressed to the person who would hire you
- tell why you are writing
- tell your qualifications for the work
- touch on the benefits you would bring to the company
- contain specific information about the company gleaned from research or networking
- close by requesting a meeting which you will call to set up
- be interesting, easy to read, and fit on one page
- be followed up by a phone call
- always accompany a resume that is mailed or faxed
- be printed on high-quality stationery matching your resume (if included)
- be mailed in a matching envelope with a typed address (no handwriting)
- never use your current job stationery or envelopes (employee theft!)

The first sentence is crucial. It must grab the employer's attention and hold it. Mention a referral or article, or make an eye-opening (or at least interesting) comment about your profession, the company, or the person you are addressing. At the end of the first paragraph tell why you are writing.

The body of the letter tells why the employer should meet with you. Keeping the employer's wants and needs in mind, mention your best qualifications for this new work and use examples of your past work, stating results, to make your points. Tell how your expertise will benefit the interviewer, department, or company. Keep your tone positive, brief, and unpretentious. Let your enthusiasm—and even passion—for your work come shining through.

Your goal is to get a meeting, regardless of present job openings. The closing should state what action will happen next: your intention to meet and that you will call to make an appointment. *Then call within two days of delivery.*

Expect to make two or three drafts of each letter. To begin, just start writing, following the basic premises of opening, body, and close as outlined above. Don't edit anything on your first draft, just get your thoughts on paper. Then go back and review your opening lines, body, and closing, and fine tune. Are you making the most important points for that particular employer? How can you say it using fewer words? Eliminate words and sentences that repeat information or are unnecessary. Stay away from long words, and avoid too much jargon. Use a thesaurus to find more descriptive words. Finally, double check for grammar and spelling, and have someone proofread it for you.

If this writing task is difficult for you (as it is for many people), or you don't have access to a good computer printer or typewriter, get help from a good professional resume service. The extra dollars you spend could determine whether you land the interview or not. If you have targeted your job search and networked properly, you will not be sending out large mailings, thereby keeping your costs down. (Refer to Part I, How to Find a Good Resume Service)

Sample Marketing Cover Letters

Dear Mr. Smith,

Most recently I supervised a construction project build-out of five retail stores, each under budget and on time. Under my supervision, a $5 million remodeling project for a major hotel chain was completed three months early and under budget by $250,000. These are the kinds of results I can produce as Director of Maintenance for Lincoln School District.

I offer ten years experience in planning, bidding, and supervision in the areas of Maintenance, Construction, and Custodial. My resume will provide more details.

I am extremely interested in this position and believe I can make a valuable contribution as the Director of Maintenance. Please expect a call in the next few days to arrange a time to discuss this possibility.

———

Dear Ms. Westin,

It is my understanding that America West Arena will be offering concierge services. Julie Banton from AMI called you last week regarding my related background in this line of work.

As Assistant Manager of VIP Services for Citibank in New York, I provided a full range of hospitality and entertainment services for our visiting international clients. The strengths I have to offer are: the ability to provide service excellence, highly effective communications, and a strong sense of commitment. Please review my enclosed resume for more details.

I believe that I can make a valuable contribution to the concierge or customer service areas of America West Arena. To that end, I will call in the next few days to arrange a brief meeting to discuss this possibility in more detail.

———

Dear Mr. Morstead,

My contention has always been that prevention is the key to successful security enforcement. This principle, coupled with proper planning and the ability to make effective decisions, has served me well as Director of Security at the Sheraton-Universal Hotel and as a Police Sergeant for the Los Angeles Police Department. My enclosed resume will provide more details.

In view of my extensive career in law enforcement and business management, I'm seeking a managerial position in security operations at Honeywell. In hope that you may need expertise of this kind, I will call to set an appointment to visit with you at your convenience.

———

Dear Mr. Gray,

Cruise tours have always held magical qualities for me—entertainment, recreation, excitement, and romance! Please consider my following qualifications for a shipboard position as Social Hostess or Activities Coordinator.

• Project a top-notch image: professionalism, vibrant personality, and physical fitness.

• Flexible in performing a variety of jobs: directing activities plus bar, restaurant, and health club management.

• Enjoy working with all types of people in social or physical activities.

My enclosed resume and photograph provide more details. I am very interested in this position and willing and able to make a commitment. Please expect a call to determine when I may meet with you.

———

Dear Ms. Landis,

NET was recommended to me by Curt Truman in your engineering department. He informed me you are actively seeking personnel with telephone maintenance or engineering backgrounds.

I have fourteen years management experience with AT&T in the areas of engineering, operations, and safety. Recently I worked on 4KC voice and data lines, high speed lines, D3, D4, D5 channel banks, NET IDNX multiplexers, and various carrier equipment. My lifelong career in the telecommunications electronics field began in the U.S. Army and continued through my 20 plus years with AT&T. As you can see from my resume, I have extensive knowledge of telecommunications maintenance and engineering.

I am familiar with your products and very interested in meeting with you to discuss opportunities at NET. Please expect a call from me to set a convenient time for us to talk. Thank you in advance for your consideration.

———

Dear Mr. Eisenberger,

After speaking with a mutual friend, Henry Izzo, I understand that ProServ is interested in promoting a professional tennis event in Scottsdale, Arizona. Henry and I have worked together in the Washington Area Tennis Patrons Foundation and the Washington Star International Tennis Championships, and he suggested I contact you.

In view of your possible expansion, you may be needing a local event director or manager with my qualifications:

• Five years as Director of Operations for the highly successful Eagle Classic of Scottsdale—a World Championship Tennis Event.

• Eight years experience coordinating major tennis events.

• Exceptional managerial capabilities and organizational skills, creative marketing efforts, and effective cost control techniques.

I am extremely interested in the position of Event Director and am positive that my knowledge and experience can be used to ensure a well organized, successful, and profitable tournament for ProServ.

Please review my enclosed resume for more details. I will be in Washington within the next few weeks and would welcome the opportunity to meet with you. I will call next week to schedule a meeting, or please feel free to contact me. Thank you for your time and consideration.

———

Dear Ms. Sloane,

Upon recommendation of Mary Tubbs at the Department of Economic Security, I am submitting my outline of qualifications for the position of buyer.

Purchasing is the first point where use of the company's most dear resource—its capital—can show long-term productivity. This is accomplished by ensuring supplies for manufacturing at the lowest overall cost, coupled with the best component for the application.

Having been both a components manufacturer's representative and a buyer in this area has given me a real advantage. In my last position, schedules were extremely short, and the supply of components for quickly ramping manufacturing volumes was critical, though always met. My knowledge and experience in purchasing, components, and technical communication has helped me be quite accurate in cost per function and manufactured cost estimating. I am easy to work with and respect the value of productivity.

I believe my skills and knowledge in purchasing and electronics could be of significant benefit to your group and Westech Systems. I will call you Tuesday to arrange a meeting to discuss how your needs and my capabilities may fit to benefit Westech Systems. Thank you in advance for your consideration.

———

Dear Ms. Greenwood,

Your gift shops really know how to captivate a customer! After visiting several of your locations, I have admired the fun and entertaining atmosphere, combined with traditional presentations. Your merchandise reflects an essence of the Southwest that is unique to your shops.

In view of your upcoming expansion, The Tristar Group may need a district manager with experience in gift shop management, opening new stores, producing high sales volume, controlling costs, and creative merchandising. These are my areas of expertise.

Please see my enclosed resume for more details. I will call on Friday to set a time to discuss how my skills might benefit your company.

———

Occasionally it's not possible to identify a single decision maker. Handle it like this.

Dear Selection Committee,

Recently I was talking with Mr. Mark Griffin, the Chief of Security of Phoenix College, and he told me the position of Chief of Security of Estrella Mountain Community College was open. My expertise is in safety, security, administration, and working with young adults. In the interest of discussing employment opportunities with you, I have enclosed my resume and application for your review.

As my resume indicates, I have a solid background in crime prevention, safety awareness, and law enforcement. I have worked effectively with young adults as a Deputy Sheriff, a project leader, and as a teacher and coach. My administrative abilities are excellent, ranging from police administration to serving as the National Secretary of the U.S. Luge Association. In addition, I possess the ability to develop positive working relationships with civic organizations, the public, and the media.

Please consider me a serious candidate for the Chief of Security. I am available to begin work immediately. When may I meet with you?

When you follow up with phone calls, you increase your chances of setting up a meeting by fifty percent!

What to Avoid for a Powerful Marketing Cover Letter

- Don't address it to, "Dear Sir, Dear Madam, Ms. or Mr." unless you're positive of their sex.
- Don't address it, "To Whom It May Concern" or other mundane generic openings.
- Don't mention reasons for leaving any past jobs.
- Don't mention salary history or salary required for the new job.
- Don't hand write it.
- Don't use a generic cover letter.
- Don't photocopy it and fill in the blanks with names.
- Don't create a form letter on your computer, then change only the company names. (You can use a letter as a base, but personalize each one.)
- Don't use it for want ads as your main job search activity.

- Don't use it in mass mailings (narrow your list through research).
- Don't close with, "I look forward to hearing from you." It's too passive.
- Don't mail or fax your resume without a cover letter. (If you fax, always send one by mail, too.)
- Don't write about what *you* want or need—focus on the needs of the *employer.*

The Want Ads

Your chances of getting a job through the want ads are roughly ten to one, or worse. I strongly recommend spending only 10 percent or less of your job search time in this area. Remember that 80 to 90 percent of jobs are not advertised, and those that are tend to be the hard to fill and attract the thundering hordes into the hiring arena.

Ads that are particularly unrewarding:
- Blind ads without a company name. (It could also be your present employer!)
- Fake ads used to pad the resume banks of employment agencies.
- Ads that sound too good to be true (they are).
- Ads for organizations or companies that advertise because they must, but really have someone chosen for the slot in advance.

However, following the "leave no stone unturned" philosophy, there are several ways to increase your chances of gaining a meeting from using the want ads. First, read the want ads from beginning to end, every day. There are two reasons for this: the position you want may be in a different section than you would expect; and you may discover new companies in your field that are advertising for other positions. Early in your job search, the want ads may be helpful to get ideas for jobs, qualification requirements, and salaries.

Tips for Answering the Want Ads

- Don't answer blind ads.
- Research the company. (Is it legitimate?)
- Find out the hiring person's name, and mail your resume and letter to them.
- **Always** write a targeted cover letter to accompany your faxed or mailed resume.
- Hand deliver your letter/resume early Monday morning.
- If you have a computer, change your resume objective to the exact position named, and target your resume to that specific position.
- Mention all the qualifications you possess that are mentioned in the ad.
- Mention the name of the company once or twice in your letter.
- Do not mention salary history or salary wanted even if asked—say you will discuss it in the interview.
- If responding by phone, have your phone script ready and screen them, too.
- Beware of companies that want to interview you in person without screening you in any way (a hard-sell commission-only job or pyramid scheme).

PART III

Interview to Get Job Offers

Congratulations! You have a meeting set up with a decision maker in your field. All of your hard work has paid off. You know you are perfect for this particular job. In fact, they would be crazy *not* to hire you! It's a cinch! Time to sit back and think about all the money you're going to make and the new car you've had your eye on.

You couldn't be more wrong. Don't make the mistake of thinking an interview—no matter how well suited for you—is a job offer, or even close to it.

In a tiny window of time the employer will make a decision about you that can have a major impact on your life. No wonder interviews can be so tense! It is up to you to make every minute and every word count. A top-notch presentation as the best candidate takes preparation, thought and time before the interview. The way you're dressed, enter the room, interact with others, and answer questions all have an effect on the decision the employer makes about you. The questions you ask (or don't ask) can be very telling, too. Dig up as much information as you can about the company before the interview and plan how to use it to your advantage. What is your proposal? Why should they hire you? What can you do for the company that's better than other candidates?

It's best to go for the job offer every time even if halfway through the interview you decide you don't want the job. By giving it your very best every time, you are gaining good practice in communicating and negotiating plus useful information about pay scales. Your confidence soars when you turn down a job offer or keep it in your back pocket for a while. In fact, when you start interviewing, it may be advantageous to interview first with the company lowest on your list so if you make mistakes, you won't lose sleep over it.

Stand out above the crowd, make your interviews stimulating discussions, and win job offers by following these guidelines.

STEP 14

Know the Company

Commonly, people wait until the interview is in progress to find out what the company is like. This is a BIG MISTAKE! The interview is the time to sell yourself and your talents. How can you do that if you don't know much about the company? Even if the interviewer is kind enough to describe the company and position in the beginning of the meeting, you are still left scrambling to convince her on-the-spot that you are the right candidate. Instead, strategically prepare your presentation for success.

Every scrap of information you gather about the company you are interviewing with brings you closer to a job offer. Use it to formulate a successful approach and make you stand out from the competition. The specific information you want to know about the company is:

Who is the company? Who owns it? Who are the major players? Who is your prospective boss? What are your peers like? How do you and your prospective group fit in the company?

What does the company do? What are their products and services?

What is the company's history? How did it get started? What have the last few years been like? Has it grown, downsized, merged, reorganized? What are the recent accomplishments?

Where is the company headed? How does it stand in its industry? What new products or services are upcoming? What are the goals?

Why is it successful? What are the key elements of its success?

Who are the competitors? How do they compare?

Who is your interviewer? How does he or she fit into the organization? Who makes the final hiring decision? Will it be a group interview? What do you know about the interviewer(s)?

What kind of company is it? What is its work style, philosophy, or mission statement? What are the corporate values?

What are the current problems and challenges? What is the biggest challenge facing the company now? How can you help solve it?

Find out the answers to these questions from information you have already gathered plus additional information from the following sources.
- Anyone that works in the company (use your network)
- The reference section of a major library—peruse directories, search for recent articles in trade journals, magazines, and newspapers
- The company's sales and marketing materials (from its sales, marketing, or public relations office)
- Company newsletters, personnel handouts
- The company's competitors
- The company's suppliers and customers
- Visit the company's plants, stores, outlets, or branches
- Inspect the company's products closely, compare to the competitors

STEP 15

Dress to Impress

You don't get a second chance to make a first impression! First impressions are based on style, manners, confidence, and communication, but the very first and strongest impression is your appearance. Make yours a positive one. Now is not the time to be radical or prove a point. (Unless the point is that no one will hire you with green hair or outlandish clothing.)

Dress as your new boss would dress to attend an important meeting. A conservative suit, freshly dry cleaned, is your best bet. Blue collar positions may be an exception. Again, dress as your boss would dress. Take a close look at every detail from head to toe, including shoes, tie, and stockings. Have two complete interview outfits ready to go at a moment's notice. Hair should be recently cut and styled, nails manicured. Skip the perfume and after shave, and wear only conservative jewelry. Remember that you are applying for a job, not a date!

A great way to know how the people dress at the company you're interviewing with is to park outside their building at closing time, or lunchtime, and watch everyone come out. (Be careful that you don't do this on a Friday that is Casual Day.) Are they dressed casually or in suits? Are they conservative or contemporary? Can you pick out the management staff? Check out everyone's demeanor. Are they happy? Are they working late or leave right at five? Do they look like people you want to fit in with?

Looking your best will make you feel your best and give you a little boost of confidence. Have a friend with tasteful style critique your interview outfits while you wear them (even down to the shoes, socks or stockings, tie and jewelry). If your clothing is too old, too tight, too short, or flamboyant, change it, or invest in a new appropriate outfit. It can make or break the interview.

When you make a favorable first impression with the interviewer, you will bask in the warmth of goodness. Your presentation will begin from a higher platform, making it easier to reach the top level.

Recovering from a poor first impression is nearly impossible.

STEP 16

Practice the Interview

There are hundreds of questions the employer can ask. How can you possibly prepare for that? Fortunately, every question the employer could possibly ask boils down to three real questions. If you can answer these, you can answer any other versions you may be asked.

The three real questions or concerns in the interview:
   1. What value do you have to offer?
   2. Why did you choose this company?
   3. What kind of person are you?

Can you answer the first one?
1. What value do you have to offer?
The value you can offer is what the interviewer is trying to discover by asking about your past work. Apply your top skills and characteristics to the specific needs of their company. Why should they hire you? What makes you stand out from ten other candidates? What benefits do you bring to the company? For every answer be prepared to "prove it" with an example from your past experience.

The employer will hire you if you convince him that the value you produce is greater than your paycheck.

Your value will have something to do with increasing the bottom line: You will make money, save money, save time, or improve the products and services.

2. Why did you choose this company?

The interviewer's company or department is special. It provides a unique service or product. If you know why it's special, you can explain why you chose this company. The interviewer wants a certain kind of person with specific skills who understands and contributes to the uniqueness of the company and its goals— not just a warm body to fill a slot. Again, the more knowledgeable you are about the company the greater your chances of getting a job offer, and the greater your chances of finding a company that fits *you*.

3. What kind of person are you?

Does your personality fit in with the company? Are you trustworthy and dependable? What are your values and principles? How will you contribute to the company's philosophy and goals? Will you work well with peers, employees, and management? Do you have energy, motivation, communication skills, determination, and confidence? Everything you say and do will answer these questions.

There is one more question the employer will ask: **How much money do you want?**

This topic should not be discussed until strong hiring interest—or preferably a job offer—has been tendered. If it comes up too early, change the subject by saying, "I'd like to learn more about the position before we discuss salary. Can you tell me about...?" (Salary negotiation is discussed in Step 19.)

Practice answering the three key questions: What value do you have to offer? Why did you choose this company? What kind of person are you? Then make a list of the ten questions you think the interviewer will ask you, plus three very tough questions you may be asked about difficult situations such as being fired, disagreements with your former boss, long gaps in work history, and changes of career.

'Rehearse your answers out loud in front of a mirror. For best results role play with another person.

Commonly Asked Interview Questions

Tell me about yourself.

This is the number one most commonly asked "question." Treat it as an opportunity to take charge and steer the interview onto favorable ground. The interviewer wants to know how you will handle such a broad subject, or they haven't come up with a better opening question. Recite the world's shortest personal history, then talk about your work. Tell about your passion for this kind of work, why you want to work for this specific company, and two or three of your best qualifications—an elaborate edition of your 30-second commercial. Limit your response to three or four minutes. Of course, your answer is geared toward the interviewer's hot buttons, which you have uncovered in your research.

- What value do you have to offer?
- What are your greatest strengths/weaknesses?
- What are your future plans?
- Why should I hire you?
- What is your best accomplishment? Worst failure?
- What did you like most/least about your last job?
- What do you like most/least about this job?
- Name your top three skills. Give examples of using them.
- If you could change anything about your last job what would it be and why?
- Why are you changing careers?
- What tools, machines, equipment are you familiar with?
- What are your goals? How much money do you want to make in (one, two, five, ten) years?
- Why did you choose this company?
- Why should I hire you for this company?
- What do you know about our company?
- What do you know about our products or services?

- What do you know about our competitors?
- Why do you want to work here?
- What kind of person are you?
- What is unique about you?
- Tell me about a time when you disagreed with your boss.
- Have you ever been fired or asked to resign? Why?
- What do you consider to be the top characteristics of a (your job target)?
- What would your last/current boss say about you?
- What kind of working conditions suit you best? Least?
- What kind of people do you like to work with?
- What kind of people do you find it difficult to work with?
- Tell about when you had to work with a difficult person.

Answer each question with detailed, but brief, examples of your work and the results. Describe your accomplishments, then try to link your skills to the new position.

For instance, if asked what your best strength is, don't just say, "Working with people." What does that mean? Give a specific example from your past work that illustrates this particular skill and how the company benefited, thereby "proving" your statement. Then link it to the new job.

"In my last job as a department head, my goal was to promote teamwork rather than individual accomplishments. I was positive that overall we would be more productive. Teams were set up for certain projects and the teams were rewarded as a whole rather than individuals. The team's productivity increased 15 percent in six months. Are these the kind of skills you're looking for as an operations manager?"

People remember stories, and they document your skills. By linking your skills to the new position, you get feedback throughout the meeting, and the interviewer starts to visualize you in the position—exactly what you want to happen.

Refrain from complaining about any job, situation, or person (particularly your boss). Prospective employers don't want to hire whiners, and if they sense that you don't get along with others, especially management, it raises a red flag no matter what the circumstances were.

If there was a problem with a person or department that you must talk about, tell how you resolved it. Make sure you demonstrate that you were part of the solution, not the problem. Show how you turned a negative situation into a positive one.

If you've been fired, don't mention it unless you are asked directly. If it was a short-term job, leave it off your resume. If asked why you left the company, recite reasons why you would have left on your own. If it's a recent job that they will want to verify, then address it up front. You can provide an alternative reference from that job, or you can bite the bullet and call the boss who fired you, and tell him you've learned from your mistakes and are looking for work now. Could he refrain from saying you were fired? Meanwhile, tell your interviewer what happened in the least destructive light and how you've overcome those problems.

All questions refer back to the original three. Pause for a moment to figure out what the real question or concern is, and answer with that focus in mind. If the question is "Have you ever been fired?" it still goes back to *what value do you offer* and *what kind of person are you?* (Will you get along with the team, and can you perform this job well?)

Even if you're asked illegal questions such as, "Do you have children?" or "Are you married?" the interviewer is probably concerned that you will miss work because of sick children or that your spouse won't support your traveling for the job or working unusual hours. (What value do you offer; can you perform this job well?)

Age issues for older job seekers are often issues of: Will the employer have to pay you more than he had in mind because of your experience? Will you be as energetic as a younger person? Are you open to change? Are you computer literate?

For younger job seekers it may be: Are you responsible and dependable? Can you be trained easily? Will you stay long enough to make your training worthwhile? Will you get along with older workers? Will you dress appropriately?

Find out the real issues, and address them. Above all, don't lie.

Think Positive!

Use your favorite method to promote an upbeat, enthusiastic attitude. Try this: The night before your interview before you go to sleep, visualize yourself going through the interview from beginning to end. Start with the first moment of entering the building. "See" how great you look with a bounce in your step and a friendly smile, and imagine meeting your interviewer with a positive impact. See yourself breezing through the questions, even tough ones, greatly impressing your interviewer. Your questions are insightful, and the interview is a stimulating discussion. You're relaxed, confident, and excited at the prospect of working there. Then the interviewer says, "You were made for this job. When can you come aboard?"

Many studies have proven that positive visualization can improve your performance dramatically. On the other hand, if you think about negative issues and fears, that is what your mind will focus on. Think of your brain as a computer. If you ask it "What if I fail?" it will search for an answer and deliver it with brutal speed. Instead, ask, "How can I succeed?" and your brain will provide excellent answers. Think and act like a winner, and you will be a winner.

STEP 17

Conduct a Successful Interview

Bring extra copies of your resume, references, and network cards to the interview. Have paper and pen ready for notes. A leather notebook is just right to carry your materials. A briefcase is okay but can be cumbersome; only carry it if you need the extra space. Bring a portfolio or samples of your work if it's necessary. Have the name of your interviewer and address written down so you don't forget. Don't smoke before an interview—non-smokers can smell cigarette smoke easily and may be turned off by it.

Plan to arrive fifteen minutes early to cover any traffic problems. If you have time, make a trial run the day before. It's a good idea to get the feeling of the place and observe employees leaving for lunch or at the end of the day. (How are they dressed? How do they act?) On the way to the interview, again visualize a highly successful meeting and repeat out loud over and over, "I'm confident and relaxed, and I'll have a fantastic interview!" (I promise this helps.)

Once you arrive, relax in your car, walk around the block, or freshen up in the restroom, then walk in five minutes early. Give the appearance of controlled energy, and add positive impact to your first impression. Rise immediately to meet your interviewer or assistant, leaving your purse or notebook on the chair. Shake hands firmly (if offered), and meet the interviewer's eyes squarely, calling her by name. Good manners dictates the use of Mr. or Ms. with the interviewer's last name until invited to use their first name. It's ideal to bask in the light of a positive first impression, but almost impossible to recover from a poor one.

Gather your things and follow the interviewer to the office, letting her indicate where you should sit. In the first few minutes, break the ice with small talk such as a beautiful office view or interesting artwork. Then the interview will begin, probably with some version of "Tell me about yourself."

Or you could begin the interview. "Would you mind if I asked you a question? During my research I heard that..." Or, "Walt, in the purchasing division, mentioned the company is... That must be exciting for you. What stage are you in?"

Interviewing can be a burden on the interviewer when she probably just wants to get it over with and get back to her real work. Sometimes your taking charge comes as a relief and jolts her out of the doldrums (especially if she is doing a lot of interviews). It also helps the interviewer to remember you and gives you additional clues to the company and position early in the game. Caution: don't be arrogant; it could backfire.

It is *your responsibility* to give the interviewer the information needed to make a hiring decision *and* to get the information you need to decide if you want to work there. The chances are greater that you will have a poor interviewer than a tough one. Be prepared to take the lead, and steer the interview back on track at any time.

Maintain good posture, be alert and composed. Match your demeanor to your interviewer, but be natural. If she speaks loudly and tells jokes, then you lean toward that direction. If she is quiet and to the point, you be quiet and to the point.

Deliver what the employer wants. Throughout the interview, think in terms of what you can do for the employer—NOT what you want. Keep what you want to yourself, until you have sold the employer on you.

Be a good listener. Try to understand the concerns behind the questions. Whenever possible answer questions using examples of your work and demonstrating your ability to work with people, including results and benefits. Then link your skills to the new job. Show how your expertise can *benefit* the interviewer's company, department, or your new boss (who should be your interviewer).

Example:
Q. "What were your duties at your last job?"

A. "At my last job, I was in charge of the Accounts Receivables Department. In the last year I reduced bad debt by 40 percent, and reduced the average collection time from 60 days to 35 days, saving the company more than $50,000. Are these the kind of skills you're looking for?"

Engage the interviewer in conversation. The interview is a two-way street. You should be talking fifty percent of the time, and the interviewer should be talking fifty percent of the time. Ask the interviewer questions as you go along—encourage stimulating conversation. Learning more about the company and the position early on is to your advantage.

Questions for the Employer
- Would you describe the position for me?
- Why is this position open?
- What characteristics are you looking for?
- Describe the people I would work with.
- What results would you like to see me produce?
- What's the greatest challenge facing your staff now?
- What are your [team's, department's, or company's] goals for the upcoming year(s)?

Knowing the answers to these questions early in the interview gives you an edge—you can focus your responses on the company's specific needs. After you answer a question, end by asking the interviewer a question. During the meeting, you want the interviewer to begin visualizing you in the position. Use facts and concrete evidence from the past, but refer to the future position.

"In the past I increased sales by ___ (percent or dollars). I'm confident I can produce the same or better results here at Acme. What numbers do you expect your top salespeople to produce?"

"My accomplishments at my last job were _____, _____, and _____. If I was your Shop Manager, what results would you expect of me?"

Don't bring up benefits or salary. Before you even think of discussing these items, you must sell the interviewer on you. She must want you and no one else. That is your primary goal in the interview. While you are selling the employer on you, you are gathering information for your decision. But do not deviate from your position of selling yourself. Begin and end with that in mind. When strong hiring interest is shown, then negotiations begin. Once the job offer is made, you are free to decide if you want to work at that company. By this time, the interviewer is sold on you, she wants you, she must have you—an ideal position to negotiate from.

If the interviewer directs the conversation to salary and benefits, steer it back to the position and how you would fit it until she is sold on you—or as near as you can get.

"Before we discuss salary, I'd like to know more about your expectations. If I was your graphic designer, what projects would I begin with, and what accomplishments would you expect from me in the first six months?"

Listen closely to the answer, then respond with how you would handle the position, documenting your statements using successful examples from your past.

Close the Sale

Closing is one of the most important segments of your interview. When the interviewer asks if you have any questions, that is the signal the meeting is drawing to an end. If you haven't done so, ask your prepared questions and any others that arose during the interview. Then...

Recap the requirements of the job, matching them with your qualifications. Summarize the strengths and benefits you would bring to the company. Provide your list of references and add a closing statement. Here are some examples.

"I believe I'm qualified for the job. What do you think?"

"How do you think I would fit in with the group?"

"I think I have what it takes to do this job, don't you?"

"This has been an exciting meeting for me. This is a job I can do well and contribute to your goals. What's the next step?"

"I want the job. I'm available immediately (or in two weeks). Does that fit with your time frame?"

"When will you make a decision? Is now a good time to schedule another interview?"

"Is there anyone else I should meet before a decision is made?"

Depending on the position, the hiring decision could be made after one interview or five. It's a good idea to find out the process, so you know what to expect and can plan your strategy. Don't commit to salary or benefits early in the game—you could lose thousands of dollars that way. Ride it out until the end when you're sure the employer wants you.

Aim for the job offer, even if you have decided against this particular job. It's excellent practice, it provides salary information, and it could lead to a different position or a referral. Once a job offer has been tendered, always delay your final decision for a minimum of twenty-four hours (see negotiating for top pay). If you decide it's not for you, your ego will enjoy a boost from turning down a job offer.

The ideal situation is to have several offers to choose from. On the average, one job offer is tendered for five interviews. To have a choice of two or three offers, you need ten to fifteen interviews scheduled within a short period of time! However, strategic job search planning—as outlined in this book—can net you more interviews and offers than the average. After each meeting, evaluate your strengths and weaknesses, and decide how to improve your presentation.

Immediately after your interview, before you drive away (and forget), make notes about your meeting. Note the name and correct spelling of your interviewers (collect their business cards in the interview) and any personal information. What were the major points of the discussion? The key responsibilities of the position? The main challenges facing the department or company? What did they like best about you? What do you wish you would have said, but didn't? What did you say, but wish you hadn't? What is the next step?

STEP 18

Follow-up with Proven Strategies

Most employers do not hire the first competent person they interview. They may interview five to fifteen people for the same position, but their memory fades, and they confuse you with others. Your excellent resume will help them to remember you. Ensure that you are uppermost in their mind by following up with these simple, but seldom used methods.

The Absolutely Crucial Follow-up Letter

Just when the employer is sifting through her thoughts about the right candidate for the position, she receives a well-written letter from you. It refreshes her memory of you and how well qualified you are for this position. It's another opportunity to add to your positive, professional impression.

The follow-up letter is not a new idea. But fortunately for you, the vast majority of job seekers completely ignore this step. Most after-interview letters—if used at all—are sappy little handwritten notes. Those are good for networking but not appropriate at this crucial time. You need a business letter.

That very evening after the interview, compose your letter, and type it neatly on your personal letterhead. Refer to key points in the meeting, summarize your qualifications and the benefits you bring to the company. Show enthusiasm for the position. In the closing, ask for the job or another interview. Even though it's a business letter, it doesn't have to be stuffy—let your passion for the work and your personality come shining through, as in the following examples.

Dear Mr. Calligan:

I sincerely enjoyed our stimulating conversation today and thank you for spending so much time with me. As a result, I am extremely interested in the position as your executive assistant.

I strongly believe that I'm the best candidate for the position because, not only do I have the necessary technical skills, but more importantly, we share the same philosophies which nurture an excellent working relationship. My resourcefulness, professional demeanor, ability to anticipate and facilitate your needs, and experience in working well with high-caliber customers round out my qualifications. I'm confident I can make a substantial contribution to your goals, the department's goals, and the corporation's goals.

In short, I want the position. When can I start?

———

Dear Ms. Brown,

I am extremely interested in the position of Buyer we discussed today. I am positive that my knowledge and experience in analyzing selling trends, familiarity with gift shop merchandise, and working with vendors to get the best price and availability, can contribute to the continued profitability of your existing stores and help insure success for the expansion of six new stores. As you know, I have participated in opening eight new stores within a year in my current company, all on schedule.

Since you asked how vendors would describe me, I have enclosed the names and numbers of two vendors I worked with if you would like to call them. In view of our discussion, I would like to meet with Ms. Anderson personally, and will call to schedule a convenient time.

In the case of multiple interviewers, mention each person, and address it to the main interviewer. *Mail your letter within 24 hours of the interview.* If the hiring decision will be made in the next few days, hand deliver the letter the next day. If you can casually "drop in" to see the interviewer, stop in for a few minutes and deliver your letter personally.

Follow-up with a Phone Call

If you have not heard from the interviewer after three or four days, call. If the decision is being made sooner than that, call before the decision deadline. Reiterate your enthusiasm for the position, and ask when a second interview may be scheduled. If the decision is being made without more interviews, ask what you must do to get the job.

If you have followed up with a letter and phone call and haven't heard from the employer after the decision deadline, then call again to see if the decision has been made. Sometimes the decision is delayed and you need to keep in touch. If the employer decided to hire someone else, ask if she knows of any other department or company that may need someone like you.

Occasionally, the company's first choice person doesn't work out or accepts another offer at the last minute. If you were second choice, the employer may call you back into the arena.

Accept the fact that you will receive occasional rejections—it's a natural part of the process. Remember, every "no" brings you closer to a **"YES!"**

STEP 19

Negotiate for Top Pay

"What are your salary requirements?" A difficult question for most of us. Can you answer effectively?

You can be eliminated by naming a figure that's too high or too low early in the game. Or you could end up working for well below the salary you could have had. Remember, the interviewer's job is to get the best candidate at the lowest price. Your job is to negotiate the highest price for your talents. Ideally, you must make the company want you, then get the employer to name the first figure.

The best—and only—time to discuss salary is after a job offer is made or strong hiring interest is shown. You MUST sell the employer on YOU first. This is critical! Until the employer is sold on you, avoid discussing salary at all costs. If you must fill out an application before the interview that has a blank for salary required, write "negotiable." If you are asked early in the interview what salary you want, say that you'd like to know more about the job before you discuss salary, and tactfully change the subject by asking the interviewer a question. (See questions for the employer in Step 16, Practice the Interview.)

If you're asked about your past or present salary, don't name a figure if at all possible. After all, what bearing does it have on your new job? You should be paid for the value you offer, not based on what you made in the past. You may have been overpaid or underpaid, and the benefits may be very different. Try these answers:

"My current salary is within industry standards. This position has different responsibilities. Would you tell me more about the results I would be expected to produce...?"

"At my last job, I had a base salary plus bonuses and profit sharing. I'm happy to report my overall pay was higher than industry standards, due to my performance. What sort of incentive plans are available here and what are the requirements?"

"My pay was commensurate with my performance with increasing increments. What are your expectations for this position?"

"My pay was less than the industry standards because I was new to the position and wanted to gain experience and competency in this field, which I have achieved. What does your company believe this work is worth?"

Keep these facts in mind when discussing money: Salary is usually negotiable. Most employers have a pay range in mind.

Figuring Pay Ranges

The best method for negotiating effectively is to know your pay range, have a good idea of the company's pay range, and aim for the top of that range, as long as it's within yours. Expressing salary in a range allows room for negotiating. Benefits should also be considered in negotiations.

Figure the minimum salary you would accept for your job target, and add ten percent. Realistically, what is the highest salary you could expect to be paid? This is your pay range. It's easy to come down, but impossible to go up.

How do you know the company's range? If it's an industry or position you are familiar with, you already have a good estimate. Other clues: check with the library to find salary by occupation, get salary information from previous interviews, ask your networking contacts what the range is, and find out the salaries of positions above and below the position you seek. Isn't it worth the effort to make an extra couple thousand dollars? And that's for the first year.

Your knowledge of the company can pay off in a big way during negotiation. What is the company's gross annual income? What is its growth status? How does your position fit into the organizational chart?

Now you're prepared and ready. You know your salary range and the company's. The employer is very interested in you and asks what pay you need. Let's say you've determined the company's range is about $35,000 to $40,000. You've set yours at $37,000 to $42,000. If you can get them to name a salary first, it's to your advantage. The rule of thumb is the first person to mention a figure has the weaker position.

If the employer asks: "What salary do you require?" or "How much are you looking for?" or "What kind of salary are you worth?" answer in this manner:

"First, let's see if I understand the position completely." Proceed to describe your understanding of the job's normal routine including the scope of authority and responsibilities, with special attention to how you fit the position. Seek the interviewer's feedback and agreement. "Did I cover everything? Is that how you see it?"

When that's agreed upon, then ask, "What figure did you have in mind for someone with my experience and background?" or "What salary range does the company have in mind?" Try to get him to name a figure first. Play hard ball.

He will probably name a lower figure first. "I believe you are above average, but I need to stay within our budget, and still allow for raises down the road. The median salary for this position is $38,000."

Never accept the first offer, but don't turn it down. The figure is in your range. Now is a good time to review benefits to see if any adjustments need to be made. Full medical insurance, paid vacations, holidays, and other benefits can add up to 25 to 30 percent of your salary.

It's important to know if you are being offered a job or if the interviewer is just fishing. If the interviewer wants you to commit to a salary, he should commit to an offer. In the situation above, the employer has not made an offer. He simply stated the job pays $38,000. He didn't say, "Would you take it for $38,000?" One way to get him off the fence is to ask, "Are you making a job offer?" or, "If you are offering me a job, I would be happy to discuss a specific salary." or, "Do you believe I'm the right person for the job?" Of course, the employer may want to know the bottom line for several candidates before he makes a decision, but at least you'll know where you stand.

Final Negotiating Points

"Is there flexibility in that figure?"

"Could more be justified in view of [name your best selling point]?"

"The figure is lower than I expected, but I am very interested in the position. I need to think it over."

"$40,000 would be in the ballpark."

"Is $_____ within the budget?"

If you must name a figure first, your answer should sound something like, "In view of my expertise with _____ and the results I can produce in the _____ area, I believe a salary in the low 40s would be appropriate."

After you name a figure, BE SILENT, *no matter how long the silence.* Wait for the interviewer to speak. What is the reaction? Did he accept it with a straight face? Hold your ground even if he says it was more than the company was prepared to spend. Ask, "What did you have in mind?"

After considering the value of the benefits and negotiating for the best package, if you feel the salary is too low, respond with, "I understand you can't raise the salary. I need a few days to consider it." Or, as the last resort, ask "Would you be willing to review my salary after 90 days?" Caution: If you have an agreement for a salary increase or review or unusual terms, be sure to get it in writing at the time of hire.

Once an offer has been made, it's to your advantage to delay your final decision for a minimum of twenty-four hours. Why? It puts the ball in your court and changes the situation completely. YOU are the one making the decision, not the employer.

This is also the very best time to get a raise! If you have done your job right, the company is SOLD on you. The department wants you. Your future boss must have you. Now is your strongest negotiating period. Choosing a job is a major decision, and you should take some time to think it over and consider the benefits.

"Thank you for the offer. I appreciate it, and I'm impressed with this company. I'd like to think it over for a few days. Can I get back to you on Monday?"

Your potential employer will not think less of you. The company wants a savvy business-like employee. In fact, your confident opinion of your high self-worth may raise the employer's, as long as you don't appear arrogant. He may flat out ask "What will it take?" or make a higher offer.

When responding, (then or later by phone) try to boost the offer. "I'm extremely interested in this position and would like to accept. It's just that the salary is lower than I expected. I'd be willing to accept $39,500 to start. Is that acceptable to you?"

Never say you are considering other offers if it's not true—that old ploy doesn't work. If you are, don't mention it unless asked. This is also the best time to go on other interviews—with a job offer in your pocket. You will exude confidence!

Negotiating for top pay is an art. You must go with your instincts and judge your personal situation to determine the best way to handle it. It helps a great deal to have a couple practice interviews under your belt. To summarize, know your minimum salary requirement (keep it to yourself), know the company's pay range, don't accept the first offer, and delay the final decision for at least twenty-four hours.

Of course, none of this works unless the company is sold on you and you are sold on it. And that, my friend, is why you do everything else in this book.

STEP 20

Keep Your Job

There is no job security.

The idea of job security is as obsolete as telegrams and turntables. We cannot expect to stay in a company for life—or even one year—in exchange for loyalty. The world of work has gone through dramatic changes and is continuing to do so. We must also change or be forever lost in the past.

We must change our outlook and adopt new ways to survive and be successful in the new world of work. Instead of working "for" a company, we must "join" our company, peers, and customers in improving productivity, producing results, and achieving common goals. Our career and work are our own responsibility.

There is security in being loyal to yourself—performing work you are passionate about and being the best that you can be. Don't work for a paycheck—work to make a contribution and get paid for your performance.

Worklife Success Steps

Keep a journal of your accomplishments (both work and personal). This helps you keep a positive mental attitude and is useful for performance reviews, changing jobs, and identifying skills.

Inventory your skills every six months or annually. Review your accomplishments journal, and list your new skills and higher levels of continuing skills.

Find out the goals of your company and department. Amazingly, many workers don't know the company's and department's goals, because they aren't shared. Make it your priority to know.

Formulate how to contribute to the goals using your skills. In your job, how can you best apply your skills to the goals? How can you contribute more than what is expected? Can you use your skills in other areas of the company such as special events, charity drives, setting up a company child care or fitness center, recycling or environmental projects?

Share your ideas and plans with your manager, peers, and employees. Let people know what you want to do, get their feedback, make changes in your plan if necessary, and get others involved when appropriate.

Carry out your plan. When you begin an action, you're halfway there. If it's not working according to plan, don't give up. Be flexible and change your plan so it will work.

Learn new skills and gain knowledge by taking classes and seminars offered by your company, universities, and community colleges. Read trade journals, books, and magazines to keep abreast of new developments in your field. If this literature doesn't interest you, perhaps you are in the wrong line of work.

Stay in touch with your network by letting people know what you are doing, and thank them for their help in your job search. Continue to use your networking skills to build and maintain relationships with current and new contacts. Make it a point to have lunch once a week with someone you haven't seen for a long time.

Take responsibility for your own job productivity. Add value, be adaptable, commit to continuous learning, create meaningful work, and operate from passion instead of fear.

In the end there is only one thing: You must obey your heart. Do the work you feel passionate about, and live with joy.

APPENDIX A

What Do You Want to Be?

Not sure what you want to do? Welcome to the club. In my estimation, about half of the people looking for jobs can't answer the question, "What kind of work do you want to do next?" So they apply for a variety of jobs, answer all kinds of want ads, and try to get interviews hoping to discover along the way something that will fit them. Soon, the bills mount, and they become frantic, so they end up in a job far below their ability (or continue with their current frustrating job) and slowly, quiet desperation sets in.

Meanwhile, those focused people who target their job search and work diligently toward their chosen destination in a systematic way are the ones who get the better jobs faster. Are they lucky? Luck favors the prepared mind.

Three Keys to Find a Better Job Faster
1. Target your job search.
2. Market yourself successfully.
3. Interview to get job offers.

This section of *JOBFINDER* will guide you through the mystical maze of determining what you want to do. If you have any doubts or want to change careers, you must do some work to identify the right job and career for you. Taking the time to do this now will save you time overall and make your job search seem more like an *adventurous opportunity* than a depressing drudgery. Do yourself a big favor (and your boss, co-workers, family, and friends)—do the necessary work, and spend the time to select a rewarding job and career designed especially by you.

One way to decide what you want to do next is to identify your best and most enjoyable skills plus the industries that fascinate you. Imagine these as large billboards pointing to your next job.

Your Top Skills
+ Your Favorite Industry
= Your Next Job

Each step will help ferret out your true skills regardless of past work history or education. These skills applied to your favorite industry will describe your next job. By following these steps, you'll identify your skills positively with proof to back them up (to use in your resume and during interviews). You'll be confident in **your choice** of vocation, and your job search will be transformed into an enriching, positive life experience.

Let's begin.

STEP A

Make a Master Activity List

The master activity list is a list of your past jobs, volunteer work, community service, education, leisure and home activities, and organizations you have belonged to. It is not intended for employers—this is your personal record. It's important to analyze all activities—leisure, volunteer, educational, and professional—especially if you've been unhappy in your past jobs or don't have recent work experience. You'll discover clues from other areas of your life about what kind of work is best for you. Later on we will choose relevant activities from this information to highlight in your targeted job search.

On a clean sheet of paper, or using your computer, write MASTER ACTIVITY LIST. Form a column on the left and, starting with the present and working backward, list your jobs with the position, company, years worked, and city and state. The larger right column will be for activities, but leave it blank for now.

Master Activity List	
Work Experience	**Activities**
Stockbroker, 1994-1997	
Lincoln Investments	
Dallas, TX	
Financial Analyst, 1992-1994	
One Big Bank	
Houston, TX	
Senior Auditor, 1989-1992	
One Big Bank	
Houston, TX	

Work Experience	Activities
Auditor, 1987-1989 One Big Bank Denver, CO	
Asst. Manager, 1985-1987 Mom's Home Cooking Kansas City, KS	

For the education portion of your Master Activity List, list any degrees you've earned including school, city, state, and year completed. Then list all other classes, seminars, training, and licenses. In the case of a degree or license, only the year completed is needed. Other training or education can be quantified by listing the time frame of the education. Here are some examples:

Education	Activities
MBA, Finance Boston University, Boston, MA, 1996	
BS, Computer Science Indiana University Northwest Gary, IN, 1990	
ASEE, Electronics DeVry Technical Institute Phoenix, AZ, 1982	
Architecture Major University of Oregon Portland, OR, 1987-1989	

Seminars & Training   **Activities**

Management Training
Acme Training Inc.
Madison, IL, 1992-1993

California Real Estate
Broker License, 1994

Watercolor Painting
Maxwell Art Institute
Columbus, OH, 1996

Have you ever performed a community service? Have you been an officer or committee chair in a volunteer organization? These positions can be valuable assets in your job search—building skills, experience, and contacts. List your volunteer work and community service next. Add a note telling why you volunteered for this organization—it is an insight into what really matters to you. If you're an inactive member of an organization, list it in a later category.

Volunteer Work / Community Service

Position, Organization   **Activities**
Tutor
Literacy Volunteers
Chicago, IL, 1994-present

I feel strongly about helping people learn to read. It's my contribution to literacy.

PTA President
Red Mountain H. S.
Boise, ID 1995-1996

I wanted to do my part to help provide a good education for my children and others.

Position, Organization	Activities

Toastmaster (CTM)
Toastmasters International
President 1996
VP Membership 1995
member since 1993

I joined to learn how to speak in public, then became an officer to help others do the same.

Coach
Little League Baseball
Omaha, NE 1991-1995

Sports teaches discipline, teamwork, and healthy competition, plus it's good exercise. I'd rather see kids in sports than on the streets, so maybe this helps.

Other examples of organizations, associations, and affiliations that you are or have been a member of are listed below. If you were an officer, worked on a committee, or contributed more than simply being a member, list that also. If it was an organization that you were very involved in and enjoyed a lot, then list it under, "Volunteer Work/Community Service" and we'll explore it more. Examples:

Organizations, Associations, Affiliations

American Translators Association, 1994-present
New York State Counseling Association, 1992-present
Laser Institute of America, 1992-1995, Treasurer 1995
Institute of Electrical Engineers Inc., 1991-present
National Association of Accountants, Board of Directors
    1992 -present

Next is the leisure and home activity section. This is important because it may help you determine a new career path and identify more skills, particularly if you have limited work experience, are changing careers, or just starting in the world of work. Think hard about the things you do at home and in your free time. Many of these activities and hobbies come so naturally to you that you may not think to mention them. Examples:

Leisure and Home Activities

- Plan and organize group camp trips, family events, vacations, or entertainment
- Nurture and maintain landscaping and gardens
- Provide arts and crafts activities for children
- Finish the basement, remodel, or decorate the house
- Balance the checkbook and make investment decisions
- Manage the family's lifestyle with a very limited budget
- Prepare gourmet meals or specialty foods
- Expert seamstress, auto mechanic, organizer, family nurse
- Hobbies and expertise: rock hound, wilderness backpacker, model airplane builder, history buff, photographer, furniture maker, antique collector, car restoration, jewelry maker, arts and crafts, dog breeder and trainer, proficient in a sport, etc.

STEP B

Describe Your Activities

Now let's go to the beginning of your Master Activity List, and write down the main activities of the first job. Then go to the next job, and continue down your list filling in the activities of each job. Include significant volunteer work and leisure/home activities. Your list should look something like this:

Position	Activities
Office Manager Valley Medical Group Phoenix, AZ 1994-present	Oversee Accounts Receivables, Accounts Payables, insurance claims. Balance the checkbook, make deposits, buy office supplies, hire and train administrative office personnel, liaison between the doctors and staff.
Sales Rep ABC Electronics Denver, CO 1990-1994	Call on current customers, develop new customers, increase sales, provide excellent customer service, prepare accurate paperwork.

Volunteer Work	Activities
Activities Coordinator Shea Middle School 1993-1994	Plan and carry out extra-curricular activities throughout the school year, maintain budget, solicit volunteers, organize meetings, keep detailed notes.

Leisure/Home	Activities
Collect and restore antiques 1988-present	Study publications about the value of antiques, shop garage sales, flea markets, and estate sales. Strip, repair, and refinish furniture. Restore antiques as close to original as possible.

Continue until you have listed the main activity of your jobs, volunteer work, and significant leisure/home activities you have done *within the past ten to fifteen years*. Basically, most employers want to know what you've been doing in your recent past— not your life history. Your Master List will be handy if you need the earlier information and should be an ongoing permanent record.

Do it now, please.

Identify Your Accomplishments

When asked about their accomplishments, many people believe they have very few or none at all! Here are some responses I've heard when I've asked people about their accomplishments:

"Oh, I work for the government. We don't have goals or accomplishments."

"I just did my job. I can't think of anything out of the ordinary."

"What do you mean by accomplishments?"

"It wasn't like that at our company. Nobody did extra stuff."

Yet, when I interviewed these same people in depth, their accomplishments were revealed time after time. The government worker came up with an astonishing list of things she did to improve her job, peppered with her job ethic beliefs. It was so good we used it as a supplement to her resume.

Rather than focusing on your accomplishments, try focusing on the activities you enjoyed the most—especially the things you are passionate about. Just by performing work you enjoy you are probably improving it in some way—thus making it an accomplishment. These activities can be from your work life, community service, or leisure time. They illustrate your *true skills*—essential pieces of the puzzle that form your ideal job.

To identify your accomplishments (and your skills), review your worksheet for Step B—MAIN ACTIVITIES. Circle the activities you *enjoy the most*. Focusing on actions you enjoy the most *reveals your best skills*, whether you are a novice or an expert. Choose the top ten activities you liked the most.

Next, on a clean sheet of paper, write a short story or description about what you did in each activity, using one sheet of paper for each activity. First describe your goal, task, or situation. Second, describe step-by-step what you did, including tools and materials you used, people who were involved, and information used. Third, describe what the results of your actions were, using figures whenever possible. Finally, list what skills you used. Think of this process like this:

PROBLEM ➡ ACTIONS ➡ RESULTS ➡ SKILLS

Do this with ten of your favorite activities. Don't forget to include volunteer work, school activities, hobbies, and work done at home. Examples:

Accomplishments/Favorite Activities

Company/Organization: Desert Dental Group, 1990-1992

Situation, Goal, Task: The accounts receivable were way too high. One of my goals was to reduce overdue accounts and bad debt.

Step-by-step Description:
Made payment arrangements in advance with patients.
Reviewed computer reports to manage overdue accounts.
Started sending out collection letters to overdue accounts when past due at 30 and 60 days.
Made personal phone calls to accounts past due more than $200 or 60 days.
Initiated court proceedings and use of professional collections agency when necessary.
Monitored computer program to track insurance submissions and payments; contacted insurance providers regularly.
Trained an administrative assistant to take over this function.

Results: After six months, reduced overdue receivables by 20 percent and maintained that level. Collected an additional $8,400 from past bad debt accounts.

Skills Used: Negotiating, keeping accurate detailed records, using the computer to track information, communicating well in potentially volatile situations, making and executing a plan to achieve a goal, training office staff.

Accomplishments/Favorite Activities

Company/Position: Sales Representative, Comtech Electronics, 1990-1994

Situation, Goal, Task: I took over a territory that had sharply declined in sales, and the previous salesperson was fired. My goal was to increase sales by getting new customers and building good relationships with current and former customers.

Step-by-step Description:
Set-up appointments a week in advance by phoning prospects and customers.
Asked in-depth questions to determine customer's needs.
Talked with manufacturers to get best price and delivery dates for customers.
Presented detailed bids to customers, making adjustments if necessary.
Followed-up to determine status of bids and make adjustments if necessary.
Followed-up after sales to insure delivery dates were met and customers were happy.
If a sale was not made, followed-up to find out why and reassess my approach.

Results: During the first year I landed twelve new accounts (two major accounts) and increased sales by 27 percent. In subsequent years, I maintained an average increase of 12 percent per year.

Skills Used: Determining customers' needs, communicating well one-on-one, negotiating, closing the sale, maintaining excellent customer relations, acting as liaison between manufacturer and customers.

Accomplishments/Favorite Activities

Company/Position: Extra-curricular Activities Coordinator (Volunteer), Shea Middle School, 1993-1994

Situation, Goal, Task: Plan and carry out extra-curricular school events using a limited budget and other volunteers.

Step-by-step Description:
Solicited event volunteers consisting of parents and teachers' aids.
Scheduled nine events for an entire school year.
Planned master details of upcoming events and reviewed last year's notes in order to make improvements.
Assigned specific tasks to each volunteer.
Kept volunteers informed through notices and organized meetings.
Identified problems and found workable solutions.
Made phone calls to members and vendors following up on final details.
Kept detailed records of costs and expenses, and recommendations for next year.

Results: The school events were planned and performed smoothly with minimal problems and were well attended. We achieved our educational, social, and fund-raising goals all within our assigned budget.

Skills Used: Planning, scheduling, overseeing a project from beginning to end, problem-solving, organizing and leading a team, working well with others to achieve a goal, adhering to a budget.

Accomplishments/Favorite Activities

Company/Position: Garage Sale Coordinator

Situation, Goal, Task: Our family decided to have a garage sale to earn extra money for our vacation and clean out our closets and garage.

Step-by-step Description:
We planned the garage sale two weeks in advance to give us plenty of time to prepare. I went through the closets, bookcases, kitchen, attic, and garage to find items. As we collected the items, we put them in a corner of the garage. The kids had to choose two toys each for the sale and old clothes. I washed and cleaned all the items, and my husband did repairs. We added a few used pieces of furniture. Then we priced everything before the sale and borrowed tables and boxes to sort things. We placed an ad in the paper. The day before, I made bold signs to draw traffic from a nearby busy street and got change from the bank. On the day of the sale, the kids had a lemonade and cookie stand. We laid out the items so everything was easy to see. Everything was priced reasonably (we had shopped a lot of garage sales). We made an effort to greet every person, be friendly, and talk about what they were interested in.

Results: We were swamped! The first three hours we didn't even have time for a cup of coffee. Over the two days we made $525! We donated the leftovers to charity.

Skills Used: Organizing a project from beginning to end, coordinating a team to achieve a common goal, following through on details, market research, selling.

129

Make every effort to write ten examples of Accomplishments/ Favorite Activities. The more information you have to work with, the more accurate your skill assessment will be. Don't be afraid to use examples from leisure time or hobbies. The important thing is that they are activities that you really enjoy or love doing. The more you liked the activity and felt a sense of pride, the better.

Be sure to fill in the **Skills Used** section as thoroughly as possible. If you have trouble with this area try these suggestions.

- Finish the stories, put them aside for a day, and reread the stories to get a fresh outlook on your skills.
- Ask friends, relatives, co-workers, or mentors to help assess the skills you used.
- Consult the comprehensive skill category section in *What Color is Your Parachute?* by Richard Bolles.

These stories are invaluable and will be used to illustrate your skills and experience throughout your job search—in your resume, marketing letters, telephone conversations, networking, and especially in an interview.

STEP D

Rank Your Best Skills

Did you know that 80 percent of job seekers cannot describe their skills adequately in a job interview? A key element for effective communication in your job search is being able to *describe with certainty and confidence your best skills, and give examples of your experience using these skills.*

Many people believe they have few skills because they think in terms of technical skills, such as tuning an engine or using a computer. The truth is we all have hundreds of skills developed from life's experiences: a gift for making people feel at ease, an ability to throw a great party, a knack for fixing things, capable of making a dollar stretch until it squeaks, a talent for telling funny jokes and stories, and much more (refer to the leisure/home activity chart).

Clearly defining your best and most favorite skills will clarify and support the kind of work you want to do next. Prioritizing your best skills will boost your self-confidence, target your job search, help identify potential employers, and assist with marketing yourself throughout your job search and interviews. The preparatory time you spend will help you get the best job you are qualified for—in the shortest period of time.

By targeting jobs that use your favorite and best skills, you will find work that is fulfilling, you are enthusiastic and passionate about, and you perform well.

Review the stories you have written, especially the Skills Used section. Add any additional skills that come to mind. Then circle the skills you enjoy the most, taking note of any skills or similar skills that are repeated. Now on a clean sheet of paper, make a list of your top five skills beginning with your best and most favorite one or the one used most often, then second and so on.

Example:

My Best Skills
1. Motivating/leading a group
2. Planning a project step-by-step
3. Problem-solving
4. Following through on details with people
5. Conducting productive meetings

If it's difficult to rank your skills, ask yourself, "If I could have a job doing only one of these things, what would it be?" Write that one down, then look at the remaining skills and ask the same question until they are all ranked.

Looking at your top five skills, note how many fall into these categories: PEOPLE, INFORMATION, or THINGS. The PEOPLE category includes working and communicating with people. INFORMATION includes performing an action with data from books, magazines, catalogues, computers, videos, audio media, etc. THINGS are tools, instruments, materials, plants, animals, and other objects. Determine which category is your strongest, second strongest, and lowest interest.

Now determine the degree of strength—is one category overwhelmingly strong, or are there two that are close? For instance, if your top categories are PEOPLE and INFORMATION (as in the above best skills example) you would not do well in a job building models by yourself all day. But if your top category strength was THINGS, building models would be more appropriate. Keep this in mind during your job search.

Name Your Favorite Industries

What type of industries interest you the most? You probably already know or have a good idea. What industries have you worked in or studied? What types of magazines and articles do you read? Which want ads are you drawn to? Let your fingers do some walking through the Yellow Pages for ideas.

Turn to the List of Industries on the next page for more ideas. Put a check mark by each industry that appeals to you. Feel free to write down industries you thought of that are not on the list, or are more specific. Review your selections, and carefully choose your top three favorite, and list them in order beginning with the most favorite.

Examples:

My Favorite Industries
1. Electronics
2. Computers
3. Manufacturing

My Favorite Industries
1. Forestry
2. Wild animals
3. Veterinary care

List of Industries

Aerospace	Industrial
Agriculture	Insurance
Appliances	Law
Animal Care	Law Enforcement
Artistic	Landscaping
Aviation	Manufacturing
Auto & Truck	Medical
Banking	Metalurgical
Beauty	Mines
Broadcast Media	Music
Chemicals	Nuclear
Child Care	Office Equipment
Civil	Personal Services
Clothing	Pharmaceutical Drugs
Communication	Photography
Computers	Plants
Construction	Plastics
Cosmetics	Publishing
Counseling	Real Estate
Education	Recreation
Electronics	Recycling
Entertainment	Restaurant
Fashion	Retail
Financial	Science
Fitness	Security
Food & Beverage	Sports
Government	Textiles
Health Care	Transportation
Heavy Equipment	Travel
Import/Export	Tourism
Home Furnishings	Utilities
Hotel & Resort	Waste Management

STEP F

Interview for Information

It's a good idea to find out more about the businesses you want to target and the type of work you are interested in *before* you begin your job search in earnest—especially if you are changing careers or industries, just starting in the world of work, or returning after a long gap.

This step is very similar to networking with one major difference—**you are not seeking a job in this step.** You are seeking career information that will help you decide what kind of work you want to do and which company you want to work for. People will be more open with you if you honor that golden rule. Getting your foot in the door through informational interviewing, then asking for a job is asking for trouble. Because this technique has been abused in the past, it's wise to use the term "meeting" rather than "informational interview." An added bonus of informational interviewing is that it's excellent practice for a real interview.

To begin this type of interviewing, review your list of favorite industries and skills. These are the areas you want to explore. Do you know *anyone* that

1. does that type of work or activity,
2. does similar or related work,
3. or works in a company that does that type of work?

Ask your friends, family, and acquaintances if they know anyone. Keep asking people until you find someone—nine times out of ten this is easier than you think it is.

It's best to set up a meeting through a referral but occasionally not possible. If you've exhausted everyone you know without unearthing a contact, you can always call the company and directly ask the person you wish to meet with. Try a career center or career counselor at a community college for leads. See the section on networking (Step 7, Build Your Network) for more tips on how to set up meetings.

Once you have the name of someone to interview, call them and mention the person who referred you (if possible). Explain that you are considering the type of work she does, or the type of company she works for, and would like to meet with her briefly to talk about it. Stress that you are not looking for a job right now, and you will only take 20 minutes of her time. Most people are glad to be helpful. After all, who doesn't like to talk about their work or company with someone who's intensely interested? Just don't ask for a job or take up more time than you agreed on. Once you've decided what you want and which businesses to target, then use these acquaintances as referrals to help set up job interviews.

Questions to Ask about the Work
- How did you get this job?
- How did you get into this line of work?
- What sort of training/education/experience is required for this job?
- What sort of training/education/experience do you have?
- What do you like most/least about this work?
- What other type of work is closely related to this work?
- What sort of pay scale can I expect entering this field at this level?
- What are the names of other companies that perform this type of work?
- Do you know anyone else in this industry or position that I can talk with to learn more about this line of work? (Try to get at least two referrals.)

Questions to Ask about the Company
- What is the company like?
- What is the company philosophy?
- What do you like most/least about the company?
- What is the expected growth/direction of the company?

- What is management like?
- What is the executive staff like?
- Who is your competition?
- Why is this company better than the competition?

Be sure to arrive on time and leave on time. After the meeting, in your car, before you forget, write detailed notes of your conversation. Did you get the person's business card? That night, compose a hand-written thank-you note. Remember, this person can be a valuable contact later in your job search.

What if during the meeting you are offered a job? Since you prefaced the meeting by stating you were not looking for a job at this time (because you have not decided what you want to do) the proper response is, "Thank you. I appreciate the offer but I'm not looking for a job until I finish my research." But you could add that you will begin your job search very soon and are interested in this position. The chances of a genuine job offer at this point are slim—watch out for scams, commission-only jobs with big promises, or starting work or training without pay.

Only consider or accept a position at this time if you are absolutely sure this is what you want to do. It's still best to delay your decision until another meeting, so you have more time to research the company and negotiate from a better vantage point. (See Step 17, Conduct a Successful Interview.)

Informational interviewing will save you time and money.

I worked with two women in the course of a year who each wanted to change careers to become travel agents. They had determined that travel agents used the skills they possessed, plus offered the opportunity and glamour of traveling. The first woman immediately enrolled in a costly school for travel agents, and when she graduated, the only position she could find offered a drastic drop from her previous salary. She ardently worked for six months to improve her commissions and position but decided she could not make the money she needed and quit, resuming her past vocation.

The second woman called the travel agent schools and figured she could swing the cost. She then met with a travel agent who also owned her business. She learned about the low beginning pay and that only way to make the kind of salary she wanted in this business was to own the travel agency or be an outside sales rep for corporations. Neither of these options appealed to her, so she dropped her idea to be a travel agent. By informational interviewing she saved a lot of time, money, and frustration.

STEP G

Define Your Next Job

Your job search boils down to two questions:
1. What do you want?
2. What does the employer want?

You must know the answer to the first question to target your job search. Without it, you will appear unprofessional and waste precious time—yours and the employer's! Employers do not have time to read every resume word-for-word or discuss career opportunities to determine what *you* want. They are seeking someone who already knows *absolutely* what they want, because that person will do a better job. Besides, if you don't know what you want, how can anyone else possibly know? (Or care?)

Imagine you are at a social gathering, and a stranger asks what your profession is. What would you say? Don't make the mistake of explaining what you've done in the past, *especially* if you are changing jobs or fields. Tell what you want to do *next*.

The challenge is that if you use a job title that is too specific, you may be limiting your possibilities. If you're too vague or don't know what you want, people's eyes will start to glaze over. When you're informational interviewing, people will help you because you admit up front you're searching for the right vocation and are asking their opinions about it. If you're actively looking for a job, but don't know what kind, you appear to be an unprofessional buffoon asking for a big favor. The answer is to express what you want to do next by industry and function.

Once you have determined your top five skills and your top three favorite industries, you should be getting an idea of what your next job will be like. On a new sheet of paper write your top favorite industry, and below it write your top three skills. Can you think of a function/job/type of work that would use your skills? Here are some examples to get your creative juices flowing. The possible job targets should take into consideration your experience, education, and desire.

> **Favorite Industry:** Computers
> **Favorite Skills:** Persuading, explaining how things work, developing rapport with customers, proficient in using computers.
> **Possible Job Targets:** Computer sales, Sales & marketing, Technical writer, Trainer or Instructor

Same skills applied to a different industry:

> **Favorite Industry:** Gourmet food
> **Favorite Skills:** Persuading, explaining how things work, developing rapport with customers, proficient in using computers.
> **Possible Job Targets:** Sales of gourmet foods, Sales of restaurant or grocery store computer systems

Let's look at more examples using the same skills applied to different industries.

> **Favorite Industry:** Custom built homes
> **Favorite Skills:** Project management, preparing and adhering to a budget, motivating a team to achieve a goal.
> **Possible Job Targets:** General contractor, Job foreman

> **Favorite Industry:** Retail
> **Favorite Skills:** Project management, preparing and adhering to a budget, motivating a team to achieve a goal.
> **Possible Job Targets:** Management position for a retail business

> **Favorite Industry:** Sports
> **Favorite Skills:** Project management, preparing and adhering to a budget, motivating a team to achieve a goal.
> **Possible Job Targets:** Director of a sporting event

As you can see, the skills identify a type of work within a specific industry. Your level of experience and education determines the level of the position and provides more specifics about your job target. For example, you wouldn't aim for a managerial position without prior experience or education in that field. The level of management can be quantified as "Upper Management..." or "Managerial position..." or "Senior ____" Using titles like "Manager" or "Vice President" may be inappropriate because a VP of a small company is totally different than a VP of a large corporation, but "Upper Management" would work for both.

Don't announce yourself as a novice by using the term "entry level," because you may be selling yourself short for a position or salary. Just state the function/industry as in, "Administrative position in a law firm," or "Travel Agent," or "Customer Service position in a hotel/resort." Better yet, call the company (or do some informational interviewing) and ask what the entry level positions are called and what an employee in those positions does.

When formulating your function/industry, choose one or two that best suit you. You may want to target two or three areas. And having a Plan B is always a good idea.

If you can't think of a name for your new function, you can always fall back on describing your skills. By combining your favorite skills with your favorite industries, you narrow your job search, effectively targeting it to an area you are excited about—while allowing you flexibility.

If you are still having difficulty in picturing your next job, try these alternate methods. Ask yourself these questions:
- If I could have *any job I'm qualified for*, what would it be?
- What have I always been interested in, even from childhood? (ask your parents)
- What have I always been good at doing?

- What kind of activities bring me the greatest joy? (Why save them for vacations or leisure time?)
- What kind of contributions bring me the greatest joy?
- What would I like to be known for?
- If I inherited a huge trust fund but had to work full time as a volunteer to receive it, what would I do?
- If I could change one thing in the world, what would it be?
- What in the world makes me the angriest? (Do something to change it!)
- What is my dream?
- What progression of jobs will lead to my dream job? What can I do now to start?

If you know the answers to any of these questions but think it's impossible to obtain your dream job, you can plan your career moves in smaller steps, starting now.

Your Specific Dream
+ Burning Desire
+ Planned Action
= Rewarding Worklife

Perhaps your dream is to have your own radio talk show, but you don't have any experience. Start with the end position you want and work backward like this:

Radio Talk Show Host ➔ Assistant Producer ➔ Administrative Assistant or Technician at a radio station (targeted entry job)

Look at the skills you have now and use your imagination to discover how they could lead you to this position or another entry level position.

If your dream is to be a radio talk show host, you must like to talk with people and ask them questions. Perhaps you could get a starting position (pay or volunteer) as a reporter for a local newspaper where you would interview people and write stories about them. Or you could practice interviewing people with a tape recorder, then once you've developed your skills, think of a human interest story or local celebrity you know, interview him, and send the tape to local radio talk shows. You could also be a volunteer for a charity involved in radio talk shows or go to broadcast school part-time. Build a bridge that leads to your ultimate goal.

Now that you have a picture of your next job, turn to the beginning of the book, and begin your job search.

Warning: If you have trouble identifying your skills or describing your next job by industry/function, you need to do more research and assessment *before* you begin your job search. If you don't know what you want, you will add months to your job search, or you will accept a job out of desperation and become unhappy and unfulfilled. The whole mess may become a demoralizing experience. Please, *please*, spend more time now for self-assessment, and in the long-run you will find a better job faster and be excited and passionate about your work.

For more help, look through the self-assessment tools offered at the end of the book. These can be ordered individually and are helpful in determining the job groups that are right for you, thus pointing you in the right direction. Remember, they are assessment tools, not a quick, easy answer to your career choice dilemma. (Sorry, there is no quick, easy *right* answer.)

Consult the Recommended Books section in Appendix B, and read good career-changing books thoroughly. Be sure to *do the exercises.* If you need more help, visit a career counselor at a community college or university.

If you wish to hire a private career counselor, beware of firms that offer to take over your job search and do everything for you in exchange for a few thousand dollars up front. Don't do it. If you need professional help, interview several career counselors who charge by the hour, and choose the one who best fits your needs and your personality.

APPENDIX B

Resources

Personal Characteristics

Accurate
Achievement-oriented
Adaptable
Adventuresome
Aggressive
Alert
Ambitious
Amiable
Analytic
Appreciative
Artistic
Articulate
Assertive
Astute
Authoritative
Calm
Caring
Charismatic
Committed
Communicative
Compassionate
Competitive
Confident

Conscientious
Competent
Consistent
Cooperative
Courageous
Courteous
Creative
Decisive
Dedicated
Detail-oriented
Dependable
Determined
Dignified
Diligent
Diplomatic
Discreet
Dynamic
Eager
Economical
Effective
Efficient
Empathetic
Energetic

Enthusiastic	Persistent
Factual	Personable
Fast-learner	Persuasive
Flexible	Positive
Focused	Practical
Friendly	Precise
Goal-oriented	Productive
Hard-working	Poised
Helpful	Professional
Honest	Punctual
Humane	Rational
Humorous	Realistic
Imaginative	Results-oriented
Incisive	Reliable
Independent	Resourceful
Industrious	Responsible
Influential	Responsive
Insightful	Self-reliant
Inventive	Sharp
Intelligent	Sensitive
Intuitive	Sincere
Innovative	Sociable
Inquisitive	Sophisticated
Knowledgeable	Straightforward
Logical	Strong
Loyal	Supportive
Mature	Tactful
Methodical	Teamworker
Motivated	Tenacious
Objective	Thorough
Observant	Trustworthy
Open-minded	Unique
Optimistic	Versatile
Organized	Vigorous
Outgoing	Visionary
Patient	Warm
Perceptive	Willing
Persevering	

Action Verb List

Accelerated	Compiled	Disproved
Achieved	Completed	Distributed
Acquired	Composed	Drafted
Acted	Computed	Drew
Adapted	Conceived	Edited
Addressed	Conceptualized	Educated
Administered	Conducted	Enabled
Advised	Convinced	Encouraged
Allocated	Conserved	Engineered
Analyzed	Consolidated	Enlisted
Appraised	Constructed	Established
Approved	Consulted	Evaluated
Arbitrated	Contracted	Examined
Arranged	Contributed	Executed
Assembled	Controlled	Expanded
Assessed	Coordinated	Expedited
Assigned	Corresponded	Explained
Assisted	Counseled	Extracted
Attained	Created	Fabricated
Audited	Critiqued	Facilitated
Authored	Customized	Familiarized
Balanced	Delegated	Formulated
Broadened	Delivered	Founded
Budgeted	Demonstrated	Generated
Built	Demystified	Guided
Calculated	Designed	Hired
Cataloged	Detected	Identified
Chaired	Determined	Illustrated
Charted	Developed	Implemented
Clarified	Devised	Improved
Classified	Diagnosed	Increased
Coached	Directed	Informed
Collaborated	Discovered	Initiated
Collected	Dispatched	Inspected
Communicated	Dispensed	Instituted

147

Integrated	Presented	Saved
Interpreted	Prevented	Scheduled
Interviewed	Prioritized	Screened
Introduced	Processed	Selected
Influenced	Produced	Served
Instructed	Programmed	Set goals
Invented	Projected	Set up
Investigated	Promoted	Shaped
Launched	Proposed	Signed
Led	Protected	Sold
Lectured	Provided	Solved
Logged	Publicized	Spearheaded
Maintained	Purchased	Specified
Managed	Received	Spoke
Marketed	Recommended	Stimulated
Mediated	Reconciled	Strengthened
Moderated	Recorded	Struck
Monitored	Recruited	Structured
Motivated	Reduced	Studied
Navigated	Referred	Supervised
Negotiated	Rehabilitated	Summarized
Networked	Remodeled	Surveyed
Observed	Rendered	Supplied
Obtained	Repaired	Tabulated
Operated	Reported	Taught
Ordered	Represented	Tested
Organized	Researched	Trained
Originated	Resolved	Transformed
Overhauled	Restored	Translated
Oversaw	Retrieved	Upgraded
Performed	Reviewed	Validated
Persuaded	Revised	Used
Pioneered	Revitalized	Won
Planned	Rewarded	Worked with
Prepared	Routed	Wrote
Prescribed		

Directories, Guides, and Periodicals for Researching Potential Employers

Business Directories

The Career Guide: Dun's Employment Opportunities Directory (Dun & Bradstreet Information Services)

Moody's Manuals (Moody's Investors Services)

Standard & Poors Register of Corporations, Directors and Executives

The 100 Best Companies to Work For in America

The Best Companies for Women

How to Read a Financial Report

America's Corporate Families

Directory of Corporate Affiliations

Corporate 1000 and International Corporate 1000

Encyclopedia of Business Information Sources

Directories in Print

Encyclopedia of Associations

Guide to American Directories

Business Periodicals Index

Ward's Business Directory

Million Dollar Directory Series

Standard Directory of Advertisers

Who's Who in America

Who's Who in Finance & Industry

National Directory of Addresses and Telephone Numbers

Yellow Pages

Electronic Resources
American Business Disc (American Business Information)

Company Profile (Information Access Company)

Disclosure Database

Dun's Electronic Business Directory

Dun's Million Dollar CD-ROM Collection

ABI/INFORM on disc

Business Index

Business Periodicals Index

Wall Street Journal Index

Also look for specific directories in your industry.

Recommended Books

General Job Search

What Color is Your Parachute?, Richard Bolles, revised annually. Ten Speed Press, Berkeley, CA.

The Right Place at the Right Time: Finding a Job in the 1990s, Robert Wegmann and Robert Chapman, 1990. Ten Speed Press, Berkeley, CA.

The Only Job Hunting Guide You'll Ever Need, Kathryn and Ross Petras, 1995. Fireside, New York, NY.

The Overnight Job Change Strategy, Donald Asher, 1993. Ten Speed Press, Berkeley, CA.

Who's Hiring Who?, Richard Lathropp, 1991. Ten Speed Press, Berkeley, CA.

Not Just Another Job: How to Invent a Career That Works for You—Now and in the Future, Tom Jackson, 1992. Time Books, New York, NY.

Guerrilla Tactics in the New Job Market, Tom Jackson, 1991. Bantam Books, New York, NY.

The Complete Job-Search Handbook: All the skills you need to get any job and have a good time doing it, Howard Figler, 1988. Henry Holt and Co., New York, NY.

101 Job Search Secrets, Claudia Jordan, 1998. WorkLife Publishing, Phoenix, AZ.

JobFinder Action Planner, Claudia Jordan, 1998. WorkLife Publishing, Phoenix, AZ.

Rites of Passage at $100,000+: The Insider's Guide to Absolutely Everything About Executive Job-changing. John Lucht, 1988. The Viceroy Press, New York, NY.

The Very Quick Job Search, J. Michael Farr, 1996. JIST Works, Inc., Indianapolis, IN.

Change of Career

What Color is Your Parachute? Richard Bolles, revised annually. Ten Speed Press, Berkeley, CA.

Wishcraft: How to Get What You Really Want, Barbara Sher, 1983. Ballantine Books, New York, NY.

I Could Do Anything if I Only Knew What it Was: How to Discover What You Really Want and How to Get It, Barbara Sher, 1994. Delacorte Press, Bantam Doubleday Dell Publishing Group, Inc., New York, NY.

Do What You Love, The Money Will Follow: Discovering Your Right Livelihood. Marsha Sinetar, 1987. Dell Publishing, New York, NY.

Do What You Are: Discover the Perfect Career for You Through the Secrets of Personality Type, Paul Tieger and Barbara Barron-Tieger, 1992. Little, Brown and Company, Boston, MA.

Resumes

The Damn Good Resume Guide, Yana Parker, 1996. Ten Speed Press, Berkeley, CA.

The Overnight Resume, Donald Asher, 1991. Ten Speed Press, Berkeley, CA.

The Resume Catalog: 200 Damn Good Examples, Yana Parker, 1988. Ten Speed Press, Berkeley, CA.

Gallery of Best Resumes, David F. Noble, 1994. JIST Works, Inc., Indianapolis, IN.

Cover Letters

The Overnight Job Change Letter, Donald Asher, 1994. Ten Speed Press, Berkeley, CA.

200 Letters for Job Hunters. William Frank, 1990. Ten Speed Press, Berkeley, CA.

Interviewing

Sweaty Palms: The Neglected Art of Being Interviewed, H. Anthony Medley, 1992. Ten Speed Press, Berkeley, CA.

Knock 'em Dead With Great Answers to Tough Interviews Questions, Martin Yate, 1992, Bob Adams, Inc., Holbrook, MA.

Self-Employment and Other Reading

Finding Your Perfect Work: The New Career Guide to Making a Living, Creating a Life, Paul and Sarah Edwards, 1996. G. P. Putnam's Sons, New York, NY.

We Are All Self-Employed, Cliff Hakim, 1994. Berrett-Koehler Publishers, Inc., San Francisco, CA.

The Three Boxes of Life and How to Get Out of Them: An Introduction to Life/Work Planning, Richard Bolles, 1981. Ten Speed Press, Berkeley, CA.

Index

Screening 84
  by employers 14, 52
  by personnel department 65
Skills 57, 65, 91, 113, 139
  describing yours
    10, 49, 94, 131
  how to identify 9, 125, 131
  how to list on resume 14, 16
  transferable 8, 22, 24, 131
Smoking 97
Stationery 26, 39, 53, 76

T

Telephone
  follow-ups 69, 76, 104
  how to reach decision-maker
    73
  making appointments by
    65, 67, 71, 84
Thank-you notes
  after informational interviewing
    137
  after networking
    59, 67, 68, 72
Time required for job search
  44, 63
Training. *See* Education, how to
    list on resume

V

Verb list 149
Visualization 5, 94, 95, 97
Voice mail 15, 73
Volunteer work *24*
  describing yours
    20, 23, 117, 119, 128

W

Want ads 42, 44, 82, 83
  effectiveness of 42, 83

tips for answering 83
Writing
  a cover letter 76
  a resume 14, 38
  style 16, 21

Y

Yellow pages, research using
  62, 133

About the Author

People said I was lucky at finding good jobs.

I never thought about it, really. I always knew what I wanted at the time, even when changing careers, and went out and got the job.

Then one day it changed. The economy turned sour and I relocated to Arizona. I was filled with doubts about my career, so I cast about for different jobs—all sorts of things! None seemed too promising, so I took the first offer that came along. Six months later, I was in the depths of despair. A grapefruit-sized knot gnawed at my stomach from Sunday night to Friday afternoon, disappearing during the weekend. Obviously, I hated my job and it was making me physically ill.

That winter vacation, I checked out twenty books from the library about job search, changing careers, soul searching—anything and everything about resolving a career dilemma. I read them all and completed exercise after exercise. Then, using the best parts of each book I crafted a job search plan. It made sense. I discovered again *exactly* what I wanted to do, and learned how to sell my talents. My plan worked better than I had hoped. With confidence and charisma, I aced the interviews at companies I had chosen.

My new jobs were exciting. First, I received a 35 percent raise above my previous job salary. Nine months later, from the new contacts I had made, I was offered my dream job of a lifetime with an additional 40 percent raise. Thrilled that my methods had worked so successfully, I began helping my friends (and my husband) find better jobs in my spare time. The job search became fun and challenging for me and my friends.

161

Alas, good things do come to an end. My dream job ended and I was laid off, *again*. My husband suggested that I start my own business helping people find better jobs. After all, I had years of hiring experience as a business manager, I had been helping my friends find better jobs, and I really enjoyed it. A business was born.

My clients loved to read the brief handouts I gave them, telling me they were very helpful, but job seekers would seldom read books I recommended because of limited time. This book is designed to be streamlined, but packed with information—all the secrets of the job search without the long, drawn-out explanations. After five years of helping individuals, I decided I could reach more people though books.

In addition to *JobFinder: How to Find a Better Job Faster*, I have written *101 Job Search Secrets*, and the *JobFinder Action Planner*.

Do you deserve to have a job you love and can perform well? Do you deserve to be productive and happy in your work life—to be the best you can be, in the best job you are qualified for? ***It is your responsibility to do this for yourself.*** No one else will do it for you. Or will care enough to do it as well as you can.

Why wait until 5 p.m. on Friday to be happy? Or until your vacation? Think of what a difference it would make in your life if you looked forward to Monday! And every workday.

Imagine if everyone was happy and productive in their jobs! Our country, our world, would hum like the high-tech computers it produces.

Order Form

Order by mail, fax, or phone!
Pay by check, money order, or credit card.

To:

WorkLife Publishing
4532 E. Grandview Rd.
Phoenix, AZ 85032

1-800-493-1585
Fax (602) 493-9321

I would like to order:

$ Amount

_____ copies of *JobFinder: How to Find a Better* _____
Job Faster @ $12.95+$1.50 postage each.

_____ copies of *101 Job Search Secrets*
@ $6.95 + $1.00 postage each. _____

_____ copies of *JobFinder Action Planner*
@ $29.95+ $4.00 postage each. _____

Career Assessment Guides:
_____ copies of The Career Exploration Inventory
@ $2.95 +$.65 postage each. _____

_____ copies of Holland Self-Directed Search
(SDS) @ $4.50 + $.65 postage each. _____

Allow 3-4 days for delivery.

Total $ _____

Send to: (please print)

Name _____
Organization _____
Mailing address _____
City, State, Zip _____
Credit Card # _____
Expiration _____
Signature _____